I0605557

More Praise for *Church Tomorrow?*

"In *Church Tomorrow?* Stephanie Spellers has given us a lively, accessible guide to the demographic and sociological trends reshaping our church and the perspectives of generations we too often fail to reach. In these pages, readers will find a spirited and timely challenge to the status quo and a valuable tool for discerning where the Spirit is leading Episcopalians and the church we love."

—Sean Rowe, 28th Presiding Bishop of The Episcopal Church

"Through deep listening, Stephanie Spellers amplifies the voices of seekers, skeptics, and spiritual dreamers too often ignored. *Church Tomorrow?* calls us to live with authenticity, courage, and love, reminding us that the Spirit still breathes new life into dry bones. May this book find its way into many hands and hearts."

—Julia Ayala Harris, president, Episcopal House of Deputies

"With prophetic insights from voices long past and the testimony of today's 'nones and dones,' Stephanie Spellers subtly shifts the question from where did they go? to where does the church go? *Church Tomorrow?* is not a portrait of decline or uncertainty, but a call into conversation—a summons to rediscover what it means to be a people called out to embrace the dynamic, passionate, and incarnate movement of the gospel. In this way, the 'nones and dones' offer us a vision for becoming the church of tomorrow. This book lets us in on that vision."

—Kelly Brown Douglas, author of *Resurrection Hope*

"Stephanie Spellers has given us so much: in-depth analysis of religious practice in America, and a chance to hear the stories of young adults seeking spiritual meaning who aren't finding it in our churches. More importantly, she challenges us to *hear* what they have to say as a prophetic word to the church. This is a book I will return to often and share with other Christian leaders."

—Mariann Budde, Bishop of the Episcopal Diocese of Washington and author of *How We Learn to Be Brave*

"Remarkable . . . a vision for the future that is decidedly *not* the way we've always done it but instead shaped by the way of Jesus and his love."

—from the foreword by Michael B. Curry, former Presiding Bishop of The Episcopal Church

"Reverend Stephanie Spellers has been a guide and prophet to me many times, and what I love about this book is that now even more people will get to benefit from the leadership, the vision, and the wisdom that has affected me so powerfully. If you're wondering about the future of the church, put this important book at the top of your list."

—Shauna Niequist, *New York Times* bestselling author of *Cold Tangerines*, *Present Over Perfect*, and *I Guess I Haven't Learned That Yet*

"Rev. Stephanie Spellers brings the fire. Just as James Baldwin said that it is his love for America that drives him to criticize her perpetually, Spellers loves the church so much she will not settle for what it has become. Through the eyes of the 'Nones' and 'Dones' she holds a mirror up to the church and asks the question: 'Is this who we want to be?' This is a wake-up call, a prophetic rebuke of religious hypocrisy, a 'get-behind-me-Satan' exorcism inside the pious institutions we call 'church.' But it is also an invitation to reimagine how God moves in the world, a liberating escape from the theological jails we've locked ourselves into, and a firm reminder that new life comes out of the compost . . . even the compost of Christendom."

—Shane Claiborne, author of *The Irresistible Revolution* and cofounder of Red Letter Christians

"Folks, this is it. This is the book for church leaders in the 2020s to read and discuss together, as soon as possible. My suspicion is that many church leaders will then ask their whole congregation to read it. *Church Tomorrow?* not only provides the content we need, shared with clarity, skill, and sensitivity . . . it also comes from the person— and people—we need to bring us this message. If you love your church, read this book as soon as you can."

—Brian D. McLaren, author of *Do I Stay Christian?* and *Faith After Doubt*

"As a millennial priest doing ministry with mostly former 'nones and dones,' it frustrates me how rarely solutions posed by the church to our own decline actually converse with people who aren't in our pews. God bless Rev. Canon Spellers for actually listening to the people the church loves to talk about, and for asking the obvious, but terribly taboo, question: Why aren't y'all here? Rev. Canon Spellers offers her incredible dual gifts as a meticulous journalist and deep, pastoral listener to paint a portrait I want everyone worrying about emptying pews to prayerfully read."

—Lizzie McManus-Dail, author of *God Didn't Make Us to Hate Us*

"Weaving together survey data and in-depth interviews, *Church Tomorrow?* offers a rare blend of depth and nuance in the analysis of American religion. Written in an accessible and engaging style, it deepens and broadens the conversation around the growing trend of religious disaffiliation in the United States."

—Ryan Burge, author of *The Nones*

"Stephanie Spellers's *Church Tomorrow?* lays foundations for the next critical conversation in the American church. With authority that comes from leadership in one of America's oldest denominations, Spellers asks two critical questions: Can these bones live? And if so, how? Combining the storytelling power of numbers, testimony, and scripture, Spellers weaves the story of the church now and the church that yet can be, if only leaders lay hold of actual faith and move the body of Christ into new ways of being together in the world. Read this book. Then do it."

—Lisa Sharon Harper, author of *The Very Good Gospel*

"Stephanie Spellers has written a book that is in part a critical diagnosis and a doxology. With candor and compassion, she chronicles congregational decline, but without lament. In fact, this book calls forth healing and hope! *Church Tomorrow?* listens to the Nones and Dones not as statistics but as sages, reminding us that dry bones still rattle with the Spirit's breath. This is a prophetic and practical word that cuts through clichés, confronts complacency, and calls the church to courage. Anyone who cares about the future of faith should read this book, wrestle with its witness, and rejoice in its vision."

—Dr. Jonathan Lee Walton,
president of Princeton Theological Seminary

"Stephanie Spellers knows the church and knows the voices of those who seek spiritual community like no one else. Her newest book is a rich dive into the voices of spiritual young adults who do not find belonging in Christian churches. This is an important read for those of us who seek to serve them from the church."

—Winnie Varghese, dean of the Cathedral Church of
St. John the Divine in New York

CHURCH TOMORROW?

WHAT THE 'NONES' AND 'DONES' TEACH US ABOUT THE FUTURE OF FAITH

STEPHANIE SPELLERS

Data drawn primarily from the following sources: Pew Research Center, Gallup Organization, General Social Survey, Cooperative Congressional Election Study, and American Enterprise Institute. These organizations bear no responsibility for the interpretations presented or conclusions reached based on analysis of the data.

Morehouse Publishing
19 East 34th Street
New York, NY 10016
www.churchpublishing.org

Morehouse Publishing is an imprint of Church Publishing Incorporated.

Cover design by David Baldeosingh Rotstein
Charts redrawn by Kristin LeMay
Typeset by Westchester Publishing Services

ISBN 978-1-64065-860-8 (hardcover)
ISBN 978-1-64065-864-6 (eBook)

Library of Congress Control Number: 2025941031

For the 'Nones' and 'Dones'—
you are always on my heart.

Table of Contents

Foreword by Bishop Michael B. Curry xi

Introduction Can These Bones Live? 1

PART I **THE GREAT DISAFFILIATION** 15

1 The Rise and Fall of Christian America 17

2 Where Did Everybody Go?: Why the Pews Emptied and the Nones Grew 37

PART II **THE NONES AND DONES SPEAK** 55

3 Becoming None and Done 63

4 Seeking the Sacred 85

5 Building Community While Bowling Alone 105

Part III **PROPHESY TO THE BONES** 127

6 Will the Real Christians Please Stand Up? (First Prophecy) 137

7 Stop Making Idols of Your Institutions, Buildings, Rules, and Dogma (Second Prophecy) 147

8 Go Meet the God Who Is Waiting Outside (Third Prophecy) 153

9 Form Loving, Embodied Communities That Welcome Our Whole, Authentic Selves (Fourth Prophecy) 157

Part IV **THE FUTURE OF FAITH** 165

10 We Are the Jesus Movement (Response to the First Prophecy) 173

11 Our Institutions Can Innovate and Liberate (Response to the Second Prophecy) 183

12 We Can Seek God Beyond the Walls (Response to the Third Prophecy) 195

13 Let's Dance (Response to the Fourth Prophecy) 203

Conclusion And You Shall Live 215

Acknowledgments 219

Endnotes 225

Bibliography 235

Foreword

The title of Stephanie Spellers's remarkable new book is a simple question: "Church Tomorrow?" Once upon a time, that would have been a statement, and an unremarkable one at that. Of course we'll be at church tomorrow. Of course our churches will be around tomorrow. None of that is a given today. There is, in our time, legitimate anxiety about and concern for the future of the Christian church, at least in the Global North and historic West. The reality of the numbers, the emergence of generations of the nonreligious "Nones and Dones," and the bleakness of future predictions around the vitality of religious faith in America are all quite real.

But as I read this book, as I listened to the stories within the statistics, as I heard the voices of young nonreligious people and really listened to and learned from them, I kept hearing a song. It is a Negro spiritual, created and sung by enslaved Africans here in America. It is a song born in the crucible of suffering and struggle. And yet, it is a powerful declaration of invincible hope that not even the titanic powers of death can defeat.

This is what they said:

I looked over Jordan and what did I see?
Coming for to carry me home?
A band of angels coming after me.
Coming for to carry me home.

Swing low, sweet chariot,
Coming for to carry me home.
Swing low, sweet chariot,
Coming for to carry me home.

The story behind the spiritual resides in 2 Kings. There the Prophet Elijah is nearing the end of his life. He and his successor Elisha have just literally crossed over the Jordan River. "As they continued walking and talking, a chariot of fire and horses of fire separated the two of them, and Elijah ascended in a whirlwind into heaven" (2 Kings 2:11).

The spiritual begins with the slave, standing in the place of Elijah, looking over the Jordan. He beholds the chariot drawing near, and the singer becomes a participant in the biblical story, only in a new time and in a new way. The singer shares in Elijah's joy that the chariot is indeed "coming for to carry me home."

Like many of the Negro spirituals, this one contained multivalent meanings, seditious messages that subverted the political and economic status quo in which enslaved people were compelled to live. While it was a funeral song, sung to mark the transition from life in this world to life in the next, it was also a freedom song, sung as a reminder that their liberation was the ultimate will, intention, and dream of God.

For an enslaved person, to look over Jordan is to see beyond the limitations of the present and to behold, as St. Paul said, what "no eye has seen, nor ear heard . . ." (1 Corinthians 2:9). Looking over Jordan is gazing beyond the probabilities of the present to the infinite possibilities of God's new future: a new heaven, a new earth. It is beholding what is possible when the words of the Lord's Prayer—"Thy kingdom come. Thy will be done in earth, as it is in heaven" (Matthew 6:10 KJV)—are answered from on high. Looking over Jordan is the work of the church in this moment.

> If you get there before I do,
> Coming for to carry me home,
> Tell all my friends I'm coming too,
> Coming for to carry me home.
>
> Swing low, sweet chariot,
> Coming for to carry me home.
> Swing low, sweet chariot,
> Coming for to carry me home.

The wonder of this book is that Spellers begins with a formidable complex of data and history concerning disaffiliation from organized religion and the state of faith in America, and she has made it accessible, understandable, and clear. That is no small accomplishment. But that is only the beginning.

Spellers intuitively knows what Pythagoras, the philosopher and mathematician of ancient Greece, knew. Behind the numbers and the statistical analysis are very real human beings with legitimate spiritual strivings and stories. This book turns our attention to them. In the powerful set of testimonies at the book's center, Spellers has chronicled a selection of the realities and hopes of America's nonreligious young adults. All of a sudden, the facts have faces, the numbers have names, the statistics are souls, and they become nothing less than our siblings, brothers, and sisters in the human family of God. They give voice to deep hopes, troubles, and questions we in the church often miss. Because of their offering, new possibilities beyond the usual institutional probabilities can emerge.

In the final sections, Spellers then creates a conversation between the people she interviewed and contemporary thinkers and leaders of faith. The result is a vision for the future that is decidedly *not* the way we've always done it, but instead shaped by the way of Jesus and his love. Walking into this future will require bravery born of deep faith. If we do it, the church could yet become a twenty-first-century version of the first-century Jesus Movement that is the root of Christianity.

Something akin to this happened when Mary Magdalene and some other woman disciples of Jesus went to the tomb that Easter morning. They went thinking Jesus was not alive. They loved him, and they wanted to make sure their loved one received a proper burial. They didn't know how they would roll away the stone. They didn't know if there would still be a guard to prevent them from entering the tomb. They didn't know what dangers lurked ahead. They didn't know, as the old saying says, "what the future may hold." But they did know, as the saying continues, "who holds the future." And so they went against the odds, hoping against hope. They went to the tomb that Easter morning. Even when it was dark, they went. And when they got there, an angel met them inside the tomb.

> But the angel said to the women, "Do not be afraid, for I know that you are looking for Jesus who was crucified. He is not here, for he has been raised, as he said. Come, see the place where he lay. Then go quickly and tell his disciples, 'He has been raised from the dead, and indeed he is going ahead of you to Galilee; there you will see him.' This is my message for you." (Matthew 28:5–7)

This was the message of the Resurrection: "Jesus lives! He has gone ahead of you into God's future. So, rise up and follow him." They and the others got up and went, and they saw him alive in Galilee, having gone ahead of them into the future.

As it was for them, so it will be for us. Like the angelic messenger in the tomb that Resurrection morning, this book is a messenger pointing us beyond the tomb, beyond decline and despair, to the twenty-first-century Galilees where our risen Lord Jesus Christ is to be found. In him we will find God's way of love and a life that nothing can diminish or defeat. In him we discover the chariot that carries us beyond death's shadow to brighter shores. Then the church will have a "tomorrow."

—The Right Reverend Michael B. Curry
Former Presiding Bishop and Primate of
The Episcopal Church
June 2025

Can These Bones Live?

I was born in 1971. At the time, 90 percent of Americans identified as Christian and 4 percent claimed no religion at all.[1] By 1998, the year of my baptism, 87 percent of Americans still said they were Christian, and 6 percent reported no preference.

As of 2025, the most recent reports say 62 percent of Americans are Christian, and 28 percent identify as Nones—which means, given a survey of religious preference, they would check the box for "None."[2]

Draw the lines from 1971 to 1998 to 2025. Imagine those trajectories extending another twenty-five or fifty years. Factor in the reality that nearly half of Generation Z (Americans born between 1998 and 2013) currently identify as Nones.[3]

Then take a deep breath and consider this: Over the last three decades, from 1990 to 2020, the mainline Protestant churches have suffered stunning losses.[4] The Presbyterian Church USA and United Church of Christ (Congregationalists) lost more than half their membership. My own Episcopal Church has made a 41 percent descent, while Lutherans said goodbye to 36 percent.

The United Methodists clocked a 31 percent decline for the same period; if you count the exodus following the denomination's 2023 split, it's a staggering 52 percent drop.[5]

If these figures don't send a shiver down your faithful spine, I'm not sure what will.

And yet, most church leaders I know don't sit for long with these realities. We all have coping strategies: introduce the next congregational development program, listen to the hottest turnaround expert, sell a building and use the proceeds to sustain struggling ministries, trade encouraging stories of growing churches, hold on just long enough for younger generations to have kids and (re)turn to a community of faith.

After two decades of ordained ministry at the congregational, diocesan, and denominational levels, I've heard and tried most all of these strategies and supported leaders determined to keep up a brave face. But recently a forty-something friend and colleague turned to me, broke the seal, and voiced the terror we try to hold at bay. "Are we the generation who will turn off the ventilator and call it?" he asked. "Are we the ones to turn out the lights and hand over the keys? Did I give my life for this?"

Even if we can point to lively churches and ministries, traditional Christianity in America has officially been in systemic decline pretty much our whole careers. We've peered into the valley of dry bones. It's our church down there.

If you've seen what we've seen, whatever your generation, please know you're not alone, and you don't need to pretend. Systemic decline sounds clinical, but the truth is that it hurts, and it is deeply personal. Decline is the parish register that captures smaller numbers year after year, adding up to decades of loss. Decline is fewer people in the pews, fewer pledging households, fewer baptisms, confirmations, and marriages. It is performing too many funerals. It is standing in a pulpit looking out at empty spaces that were once full family pews. It is ending beloved ministries because there's no one to run them.

Decline is the downward arc on a graph. It is also the curved lines on a brave, tired elder's face. I've seen them in countless churches and clergy conferences, not only among Episcopalians but across the ecumenical spectrum. I see it when I visit my hometown of Frankfort, Kentucky, where the vibrant Black Baptist and African Methodist Episcopal churches that marked my youth are now struggling to keep the doors open, or they've already given up the fight.

Decline hurts all over. It feels like a judgment on our congregations and on us as followers of Jesus. He told us to "therefore go and make disciples of all nations" (Matthew 28:19). We couldn't even keep our own children in the faith.

I believe in the resurrection power of our Lord Jesus Christ, *and* I know we can't get to resurrection without sitting at the cross. Even if your church is an outlier with plenty of money, full pews, and young people galore, you know the strong winds shaking most traditional houses of faith. The fundamentals have changed. The ground has shifted. Doing what we've always done, but doing it better, or doing it with some new people who love what we love, is no longer an option. Not when that yawning valley of dry bones looms just below. Not when you're walking through it.

This book takes that valley seriously and in turn asks a serious question: Church tomorrow? Within those two words rest more wonderings: whether you're going to church tomorrow, whether we will have church tomorrow, whether today's church should exist tomorrow, what might be the shape and makeup of church tomorrow, and what God intends for God's church and the way of Jesus in the years to come. I don't know the answers, but I do know the time to "Keep Calm and Carry On" has passed. Even talk about "decline" can mask the depth of the culture shift before us. We are past due for a reckoning about the gap between Christianity and the emerging post-Christian culture all around. I hope we can have that conversation here and now, and not just among church folk.

Because here's the thing: Christians and other religious people aren't the only ones talking to the divine, and we never have been. Just beyond the church doors, God is meeting people. They may have no religion to call their own. They may be dipping into multiple pools of wisdom and tradition. There may be no label for their particular amalgam of belief and practice, but it often smells undeniably of the holy.

As early as 2012, the Pew Center for Research began to tag these religiously unaffiliated people as "nonreligious" or "Nones." The subset who were once religious and abandoned the faith are often called "Dones" or "dechurched." A huge chunk of Nones in the United States also fall into the "spiritual but not religious" camp, where they refuse religious labels, structures, and doctrines but consciously retain a personal, experiential tether to the sacred. The categories are fuzzy, but this much is clear: Traditional religion may be struggling in our current multicultural, pluralistic, digital, hyper-connected yet deeply isolated landscape, but there is plenty of spiritual life and hunger beyond the borders of the church.

Many religious people already know this truth. We celebrate God in nature. We pray to God during yoga. We experience transcendence while making music. But we shouldn't assume we already know the spiritual lives and struggles of Nones and Dones. The paths they are walking are unique and revealing for anyone who wants to understand the increasingly post-Christian culture within which we live and move. And no one knows this emerging cultural terrain more intimately than Millennials and Gen Zers who have spent their entire lives navigating it. I can't help but wonder what we might learn by their side about the movement of the Spirit today *and* tomorrow. Might their honest insights help to call the church back to its true purpose and away from easy cultural accommodation? Might we together reimagine and embrace new forms of life?

Whatever future God has in store for Christianity, I know in my bones we won't fulfill that promise without the accompaniment and wisdom of younger Americans on the edge of the church's life.

Prophesy to the Bones

This wouldn't be the first time God sent a young prophet on the margins to speak to God's people in the valley.

Late in the sixth century B.C.E., the Babylonians attacked Jerusalem and forced the Jewish people into exile. Ezekiel was among that first group of refugees. The biblical book that bears his name opens on his thirtieth birthday. It should have been a moment for celebration, the day of his installation as a temple priest in Jerusalem. Instead, he sat alone on the banks of the River Chebar, in the land of the Chaldeans.

Ezekiel was far from home, but he wasn't far from God. Although everything in his preparation said God was back at the temple in Jerusalem, God came to him in Chaldea. The Spirit showed him a vision of four living creatures in the sky, emerging from cloud and fire. He saw a human figure made of gleaming amber and flame—the living God, not housed in the temple but sparkling and glowing by the riverbank.

God gave Ezekiel a scroll and bid him to eat it so he could speak a word of truth to the exiled house of Israel. Over time, Ezekiel saw and heard from God regularly. A few years into his sojourn, he received this vision:

> The hand of the Lord came upon me, and he brought me out by the spirit of the Lord and set me down in the middle of a valley; it was full of bones. He led me all around them; there were very many lying in the valley, and they were very dry. He said to me, "Mortal, can these bones live?" I answered, "O Lord God, you know." Then he said to me, "Prophesy to these bones and say to them: O dry bones, hear the word of the Lord. Thus says the Lord God to these bones: I will cause breath to enter you, and you shall live. I will lay sinews on you and will cause flesh to come upon you and cover you with skin and put breath in you, and you shall live, and you shall know that I am the Lord." (Ezekiel 37:1–6)

Young Ezekiel prophesied as he was told. The rest you likely know: The valley filled with the sound of rattling, then the toe bone connected to the foot bone, the foot bone connected to the leg bone . . . On and on, until the re-membered bones were covered with flesh, and breath filled them all. Once-dry, now-supple bodies stood on their feet, alive and powerful. God promised Ezekiel the vision in the valley would one day come to pass for Israel. "Therefore prophesy and say to them: Thus says the LORD GOD: I am going to open your graves and bring you up from your graves, O my people. . . . I will put my spirit within you, and you shall live" (Ezekiel 37:11–14).

Over the last few years, I've often wondered, "Can these bones live?" and found myself listening for voices like Ezekiel's. There is wisdom aplenty inside the institution, but God also needs us to grasp something many of our younger neighbors outside already know quite well. It is something deep about flesh, about truth, about community, about love, about transformation and resurrection in our time. Combine their insight with the church's wisdom and treasures, and we might all discover new life in the valley of the dry bones.

Welcome to the Conversation

That conviction and curiosity shape every page of this book. We will move together through four parts, and I hope each section inspires you toward greater wonder and wider conversation. Part I, "The Great Disaffiliation," surveys the data and history surrounding decline and disaffiliation from civic and religious institutions, along with the emergence of Nones and Dones as a significant presence in American life. It opens with Chapter 1, "The Rise and Fall of Christian America." If you're not a data nerd, have no fear. I reviewed and culled material from leading researchers and focused on the data that seemed most relevant, timely, and accessible. Together we will chart the rise and fall of church affiliation through key historical periods and take a closer look at just who are America's Nones and Dones.

The second chapter centers a painfully familiar question. In "Where Did Everybody Go?: Why the Pews Emptied and the Nones Grew," I will draw together various socio-cultural strands to better understand the forces driving Americans away from religious institutions and toward a different kind of spiritual journey. (Warning: If you think you already know, you're in for some surprises.) We will also take note of the isolating impact of media, technology, consumer culture, and secularism on all our spiritual and social lives, and especially on Millennials and Gen Z.

With that solid background, we will launch into Part II, "The Nones and Dones Speak." I spent winter 2025 interviewing dozens of Nones and Dones between the ages of eighteen and forty-four in or near the San Francisco Bay area, metro Atlanta, the Twin Cities (St. Paul and Minneapolis), and metro New York, and expanded the circle to smaller communities in-person and via Zoom. Every conversation covered the same four queries:

1. Share about your spiritual journey and what path led to where you are now.
2. How and where do you experience the sacred?
3. How and where do you experience community and belonging?
4. What would you tell the church/organized religion if it were listening?

Noted social scientists have conducted larger, more scientific studies around this topic, so I didn't try to replicate their methods. Instead, I drew on my journalism background and sought to model the deep listening I believe churches can and should engage with their own young adult, nonreligious peers, neighbors, and family members. Having now met with forty-five conversation partners, plus about fifteen more of their peers and leaders who identify as religious, I'm excited to share their stories, struggles, and prophecies to the church. You'll see lots more detail about my process and about the conversation partners in the Part II opener.

Part II is organized as a chapter-by-chapter focus on responses to the first three questions above. Chapter 3, "Becoming None and Done," corresponds to the first question about spiritual journeys and sheds light on why these generations left behind (or never gravitated to) religious affiliation and how they landed outside the bounds of traditional religion. Chapter 4, "Seeking the Sacred" reveals the many practices and pathways that help my conversation partners to sustain what is often a vibrant relationship with the sacred, the holy, the ultimate, the universe, the divine, God and/or Jesus (and yes, they use all those terms and more). In Chapter 5, "Building Community While Bowling Alone," you'll hear their responses to the third question about belonging, including accounts of deep yearning for sustained community and stories about the circles they're forming in order to nourish love, family, and spirit.

Part III, "Prophesy to the Bones," sets apart responses to the fourth question ("What would you tell the church?"). The messages may prove tough to hear, so we actually begin with an interlude about practices and postures that support reconciling conversations. In Chapters 6 through 9, you will hear four urgent, compelling messages—I've taken the liberty of calling them prophecies—from Millennial and Gen Z Nones and Dones.

Part IV on "The Future of Faith" wrestles with the prophecies from Part III. I invited a group of church leaders—many of them Millennials and Gen Zers—to sit with the messages and help me to reflect on how churches might change if we took the Nones and Dones' call seriously. Our shared insights inform Chapters 10 through 13, each of which corresponds to one of the prophecies of the Nones and Dones.

The conclusion, "And You Shall Live," sums up what I believe to be the work ahead and offers a blessing for the path we walk together. Finally, if you want to say yes to ongoing conversation, innovation, and transformation, including conducting your own listening campaign, I hope you'll visit www.stephaniespellers.com/church-tomorrow and dig into the *Church Tomorrow?* Resource, Reflection, and Action Guide.

Confessions of a Former None

Clearly, I believe the road to the future church winds through terrain best known by nonreligious younger Americans. I admit I have a personal stake in such listening. As I write these words, I have spent exactly half of my life as a None and half as a Christian.

Though Christianity was always close by, I didn't get baptized and join a church until I was twenty-six and a half. Avoiding Christianity wasn't easy, given that I spent much of my childhood in Kentucky in or near a Baptist church; majored in religion at Wake Forest University, a former Southern Baptist school in North Carolina; earned a Master of Theological Studies at Harvard Divinity School; and even worked as a religion reporter for a newspaper in East Tennessee.

I was always deeply spiritual. I still dream about slowly walking barefoot in my granny's tiny but lush front yard and talking to God. My religious friends in high school liked to say I was "the most Christian" person they knew. I was saved and publicly received Christ twice while singing in our college gospel choir. But whenever I looked at the church as an institution, I balked. I saw social control. I saw misogyny and homophobia. I saw greed run amok and comparatively little concern for the poor. I saw churches obsessively focused on sin and/or on themselves. I did not see Jesus.

Why did all that change for me? God opened my eyes and gave me Christian friends and mentors who took Jesus and his gospel of radical, self-giving love and justice seriously. Just as importantly, I reached a point where I no longer craved infinite choice and freedom in order to flourish. Instead, I felt a dawning desire to grow within the context of committed relationship with Jesus and his flawed but Spirit-filled church. I certainly can't assume mine would be the right path for every other None or Done. All I know is, God met me and loved me in the context of Christian community. I will spend my life making sure anyone else who feels that tug can discover a community where they're able to grow into the full stature of Christ and bear his radiant love in the world.

Having just completed nearly a decade serving in the Episcopal denominational headquarters, I am aware that I've now ventured as far inside as an insider can go. Still . . . a part of me will always resonate with the Nones, Dones, unchurched, spiritual but not religious—all the folks who yearn for the divine yet are rightly suspicious of institutions that talk about God and love but might just want bottoms in pews. I was once one of the anonymous, nonreligious data points I'm now studying. I feel a passion and a responsibility to find out how they are connecting to the sacred . . . if at all. What communities are they dreaming of . . . if at all? And having consciously opted out of traditional religion, what would they say back to us?

I will also confess from the outset that when my conversation partners' commentary cut a little too close, I was tempted to shift the burden back on them. If these Nones and Dones have ideas about the church's future, why don't they come (back) to church? If they don't care enough to put skin in the game, why should we listen to them? Over the course of this journey, I have come to respect the logical reasons and deep traumas that prevent some people from drawing any closer to Christian community. I have seen for myself that someone doesn't have to be Christian to share wisdom or a story that blesses us. Finally, I've been reminded of a core insight from the ministry of radical welcome: If your institution has the power, you have the privilege and the opportunity to listen to people on the margins, to dream together, and to create a space where The Other can flourish. Church folk can't expect nonreligious neighbors to trust the very institution that has wounded and alienated so many of them, even if our particular churches weren't the "culprit." Neither can we lay out contract terms: If we make these changes, then they will come. Listening and embracing transformation isn't transactional. Our deep hope is to trust the Spirit, open hearts and doors, and incarnate God's dream for God's church. Who joins? That part is up to God.

So come with me now, whether you are a church leader or member, lay person or clergy, deacon or bishop, lifer or a newcomer, theological educator or seminarian, nonprofit partner of churches or just someone curious about faith. Come, whether you live in a town, city, rural area, or suburb. Come, if yours is a large resource church or a small or mid-size congregation. Come if you're serious about evangelism, outreach, discipleship, formation, youth, young adults, seniors, and everybody in between. Come if you're lively and come if you're just plain tired. Whoever you are and however you come, God bless you for taking this next step deeper into the valley of the dry bones. May God soothe our shared disappointment and answer our deep longing. And may all the exploration and examination that follows ultimately point the way toward new life, new hope, new relationships, and new opportunities to embody the gospel of Jesus Christ in a nation that needs his loving way now more than ever.

Come, too, if you're a None or Done who's curious about church, faith, and the future. Maybe you are willing to share wisdom with us, maybe you hope to borrow some of ours for your journey, and maybe you're yearning to join and grow a life of Spirit by our side. Rest assured, I know we can't approach you as customers to be wooed or a problem to be solved. We can't assume you will just come back when you have kids—many of you were never churched to begin with. The goal is not to convert or convince you, but to walk with you for a while and learn how God is showing up in your life outside the church walls. And yes, I hope we can wonder together what it would look like to follow Jesus's lead and form life-changing communities marked by love for God, our communities, and our world.

Will there be a church tomorrow? I know there will be, but I can't tell you the shape of it, the smell, sound or look of it. We will have to listen closely to the God who asked Ezekiel, "Can these bones live?," the same God who then pledged, "I will put my spirit within you, and you shall live." We will have to re-root in God's abiding love and welcome wonder and curiosity, admit what we don't know, seek unlikely friends and companions on the road, and remain faithful in the valley. In other words, we will have to follow in the way of Jesus.

THE GREAT DISAFFILIATION

The Rise and Fall of Christian America

If you're trying to understand the waves of disaffiliation and decline washing across religious institutions—or the rise of nonreligious people across every generation alive—it's best to start with the history and the numbers. Before we venture out, please take this word of caution from someone who has lost more than a few nights' sleep over what's ahead:

1. The media and religion pundits regularly report stories of church decline, which keeps the spotlight on us and invites a spiraling, insular obsession around what the church got wrong. An equally or even more relevant story is that of disaffiliation from institutions and organizations, which pays attention to the broader socio-cultural developments in which we are caught up. We will study both sets of figures in this chapter and spend the following chapter

unpacking the social and cultural factors that made unprecedented levels of disaffiliation almost inevitable.

2. Even given the dramatic departure from traditional religion, the majority of Americans still hold some belief in the divine and spirituality. Secularization may be at work (more on that in Chapter 2), but we are *not* a secular nation. Frenchman Alexis de Tocqueville toured the United States in 1831 when he was just twenty-six and wrote that America was at once "the most enlightened and freest" of nations and "the place where the Christian religion has kept the greatest real power over men's souls."[1] Unlike other Western nations, Americans have been and likely for some time will remain a spiritually vital, faithful people. Even today, with membership suffering a steep drop, the figures for belief in God and practice of prayer have declined much more slowly. Put another way, people may be opting out of organized religion, but they're not leaving God behind. This book assumes God hasn't left them, either. That's why it's so important to listen for what the Spirit is up to outside the bounds of traditional religion.

"I still think that there is a God or some force out there, just not the God I grew up with. That God always seemed like an annoying, immature man rather than the most all-knowing, all-compassionate being in the universe."

—B., 20, New York

With these reality checks firmly in hand, we can now explore the history and numbers surrounding disaffiliation and decline, first examining American religious life from the country's establishment (1700s-1860s) into the boom years following the

Civil War and World War II (1870s-1950s). After that, we will journey into the valley and look at attendance and membership trends from the 1960s to the present, and close with predictions for the future of organized religion and a picture of the state of the Nones.

Becoming a Devout Christian Nation

The popular version of American history claims we have always been a faithful, church-going, Christian nation, and people have only recently rejected that identity and opted out of faith. This tale is a fabrication generations in the making. A landmark study of religion in America estimates that, as of 1776, only 17 percent of people in the colonies were part of a church.[2] Even though most of America's founders were shaped within Christian churches and institutions, we can't assume they espoused beliefs anywhere near what would today be considered orthodoxy.[3] Thomas Jefferson famously drafted a copy of the Bible that deleted miracles and passages he found offensive to rational minds. The founders had ample opportunity to establish a church and creed at the nation's center. Instead, again and again, they chose religious liberty.

Christian fervor picked up during the Second Great Awakening (1790–1840), when de Tocqueville observed lay people and clergy on fire for their faith. As he spoke to them, he concluded: "The main reason for the quiet sway of religion over their country was the complete separation of church and state."[4] The marriage of religion and the state in other nations had suffocated religion. The American experiment seemed to prove that religious sensibilities blossom in an atmosphere of freedom.

In the years following the Civil War, the U.S. population leapt from about 39 million to nearly 70 million.[5] Close to half of those people were members of a church.[6] By 1906, Christians made up a little over half of the population. These were boom times not only for religion but across all sectors of civic life, with the birth of major volunteer associations like the Shriners (1872), the American Bar Association (1878), the Salvation Army (1880), the American Red Cross (1881), United Mine Workers (1890), Sierra Club (1892), Parent-Teacher Association or PTA (1897), Veterans of Foreign Wars or VFW (1899), YWCA (1906), and the National Association for the Advancement of Colored People or NAACP (1909).[7]

How do we explain this explosion? During these postwar years, Americans were actively, consciously rebuilding a nation and the internal, social ties that would make it strong. In other words, we were developing social capital, a term describing the set of social networks, norms, and trust that enable cooperation and collective action.[8] Religious and civic organizations are among the greatest sources of social capital; their flourishing created the sturdy foundation for a thriving young nation.

The pattern repeated following World War II. As Robert Putnam observed in *Bowling Alone*, "World War II, like earlier major wars in U.S. history, brought shared adversity and a shared enemy. The war ushered in a period of intense patriotism nationally and civic activism locally."[9] When the victorious troops returned home, a whole nation moved into high gear. The Baby Boom boosted the population by 30 million people in one decade—from 150 million in 1950 to 180 million in 1960.[10] Social and civic organizations could barely keep up with increased membership and activity.

Churches harvested a bumper crop during this season, with unprecedented growth in nearly every phase of religious life. Spending on new churches increased from $126 million in 1947 to a stunning $1.2 billion by 1965, much of it focused on houses of faith for the new suburbs popping up across the land.[11] Gallup reports that 39 percent of Americans attended a weekly religious service in 1950; by 1956, close to half of Americans reported attending worship weekly.[12] Likewise, an already overwhelming 91 percent of Americans listed Christianity as their religious preference in 1950. That figure peaked at 96 percent in 1956.

The 1950s were undoubtedly a Christian heyday. The phrase "In God We Trust" became the national motto in 1956 under President Dwight Eisenhower. Before then, the de facto motto was *E pluribus unum*, Latin for "from many, one"—that is, we come from many origins to form one nation. Likewise, the Pledge of Allegiance—originally penned in 1892 to coincide with the 400th anniversary of Christopher Columbus's arrival in the Americas—was revised by Congress in 1954 to read: "I pledge allegiance to my Flag and the Republic for which it stands, one nation, *under God* [my italics], indivisible, with liberty and justice for all."

Postwar optimism and activity only partially explain this newfound piety and holiness. With the advent of the Cold War in 1947, America faced off against the Soviet Union in a battle pitting the virtues of capitalism, democracy, and Christianity against the evils of communism, autocracy, and atheism. Senator Joseph McCarthy led the charge to save the nation from "The Red Scare," and Americans scrambled to shore up their patriotic, churchgoing bonafides. It's not surprising that, by 1956, only 1 percent of Americans admitted to being nonreligious. If you loved God, you loved America, and vice versa. No one dared to identify with atheism or nonreligion in those fraught years.

Breaking the Ties That Bind

Even before the end of the 1950s, those fearfully woven ties began to fray. The Black Civil Rights Movement shone a bright light on America's failure to fulfill the promise of liberty and justice for all. At the same time, women—having made enormous public contributions during World War II—began to demand equal rights and freedom to control their bodies and lives. By the late 1960s, college campuses and streets erupted with protests against the Vietnam War. These movements aligned with struggles for freedom of choice and conscience in nearly every sector of American life. More often than not, the leaders seeking to crush dissent and maintain order carried a Bible and claimed to speak for God.

For their part, the young Baby Boomers rejected their parents' traditions in favor of a counterculture that flipped approaches to sexuality, marriage, drugs, music, and religion. As Wade Clark Roof and William McKinney observed in their classic *American Mainline Religion: Its Changing Shape and Future*:

> Many new sects and cults emerged, with their members wearing strange garb, practicing ancient rituals, and speaking in esoteric tongues: Hare Krishnas, Zen Buddhists, Vedantists, Sufis, and scores of other "new religions." . . . More broadly, the old civil faith that once unified Americans around the

celebration of national values and purpose was deemed by many to be hollow and deceitful.[13]

The Baby Boomers might have launched the dissent, but it accelerated with Generation X. Born in 1965–1980, this cohort of so-called "latchkey kids" had to figure out values, life choices and even dinner on their own or from the ever-present TV (and yes, I learned to make Kraft Macaroni and Cheese with Spam casserole at age ten). Generation Y, better known as Millennials, were born in 1981–1997 and raised with a high sense of self-worth, autonomy over their identity, and freedom of (and from) religion. And Generation Z, born in 1998–2013, are tracking as the most nonreligious generation alive.

Successive generations of Americans have thus been more and more willing to question authority, chart their own spiritual paths, and shake ties to institutions, including but not only the church. Clergy abuse scandals, 9/11, and the rise of White Christo-nationalism[i] have only reinforced the growing consensus

---

i I prefer to speak of "White Christo-nationalism" instead of "White Christian Nationalism" because I refuse to cede the basic point that this ideology and movement is in any way actually Christian. I do, however, agree with Jemar Tisby's description of White Christian Nationalism: "an ethnocultural ideology that uses Christian symbolism to create a permission structure for the acquisition of white political power and social control." Read his February 22, 2024, Substack article, "The 'White' in White Christian Nationalism" at https://jemartisby.substack.com/p/the-white-in-white-christian-nationalism. Christians Against Christian Nationalism goes on to say this ideology "uses the veneer of Christianity to advance its own aims—to point to a political figure, party or ideology instead of Jesus." Learn more at https://www.christiansagainstchristiannationalism.org/learn-more.

"I think there's a lot of beauty in religion, tradition, and ritual. But the hurtful, harmful dogmas, the destructive narratives, the sexual abuse and the homophobia—it makes my skin crawl."

—S., 41, San Francisco

that religion isn't especially good for individuals or society. As a result, especially since 1990, markedly fewer people have identified with Christianity, and even fewer sit in the pews, while the Nones and Dones have multiplied.

For instance, as we've seen, 96 percent of Americans said they were Christian in 1956, and only 1 percent admitted having no religious affiliation.[14] By 1972, 88 percent still identified as Christian, but 5 percent stood with the nonreligious. Those figures held steady until 2008, when Christians sank under 80 percent, and the Nones rose into double digits. As of 2023, according to Gallup, 68 percent of Americans said they're Christian and 22 percent claimed no religion (other religions held steady between 4 and 7 percent during much of this time). (See Figure 1.)

It's worth noting that Gallup's numbers are much more generous to Christianity than other respected surveys. The Pew Research Center has been tracking religious life in America since 2007, when 78 percent of Americans reportedly identified as Christian. By 2024, only 63 percent claimed that identity, while Nones stood strong at 28 percent and 7 percent adhered to other religions.[15]

Worship attendance has always been a harder sell than membership. (See Figure 2.) Interestingly, in 1940, just before the start of World War II, 37 percent of the public said they had

FIGURE 1

Americans' Religious Preferences

Percentage of Americans who identify as Christian vs. no religious preference

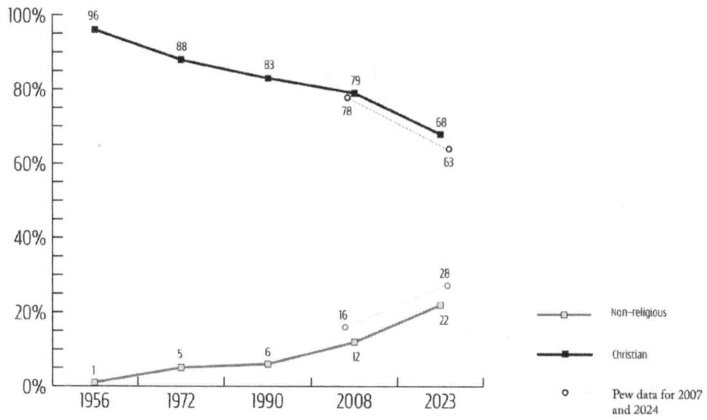

Note: Graph reflects major trends. Small fluctuations between highlighted data points not represented.

Sources: Gallup Poll Social Series and Pew Research Center

attended a religious service in the last seven days. That figure turned upward by 1958, when nearly half of Americans reported worshiping weekly. Over the next fifty years, until 2009, worship attendance continued to hover between 48 and 40 percent. In the last fourteen years—from 2010 to 2023—it dropped to 32 percent.[16] (This Gallup figure is close to Pew's report of 33 percent attendance.)[17]

As I shared earlier, mainline Protestant churches have absorbed more severe losses than any other sector of Christianity. Ryan Burge is one of America's leading data scientists around religion, and he paints a solemn picture of steady decline (he calls it a "bloodbath") in the American Baptist Church USA, the Evangelical Lutheran Church in America, the Presbyterian Church in

FIGURE 2

Worship Attendance

Percentage who self-reported attending church, synagogue, mosque or temple in the last seven days

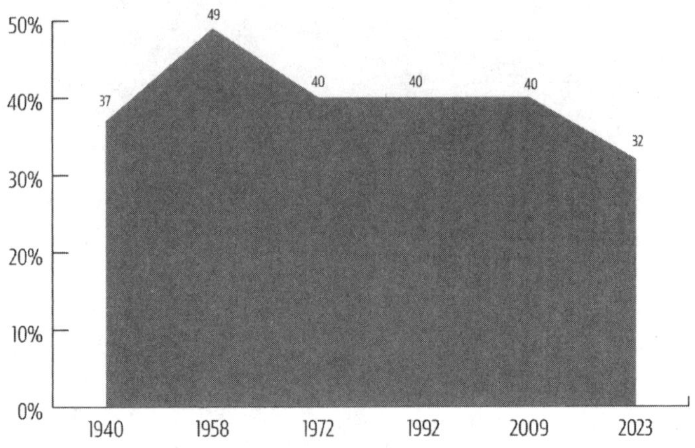

Note: Graph reflects major trends. Small fluctuations between highlighted data points not represented.

Source: Gallup Poll Social Series

the USA, The Episcopal Church, the United Church of Christ (Congregationalist), and the United Methodist Church. Below is Burge's graph depicting the devastating drop in membership from 1990 to 2020 across every major mainline denomination.[18]

Take note: Evangelicals avoided a similar fate for most of the 1990s and 2000s, but recently disaffiliation has taken its toll on some of them, too. The Southern Baptist Convention peaked in 2006 with more than 16 million members; as of 2024, they had fewer than 13 million. Nondenominational and Pentecostal churches—arguably the least "organized" group within organized religion—are currently flying high. The Assemblies of God reported 3.2 million members in 2020, a 1-million-person gain since 1990.[19]

FIGURE 3

The Decline in Membership of Six Mainline Traditions

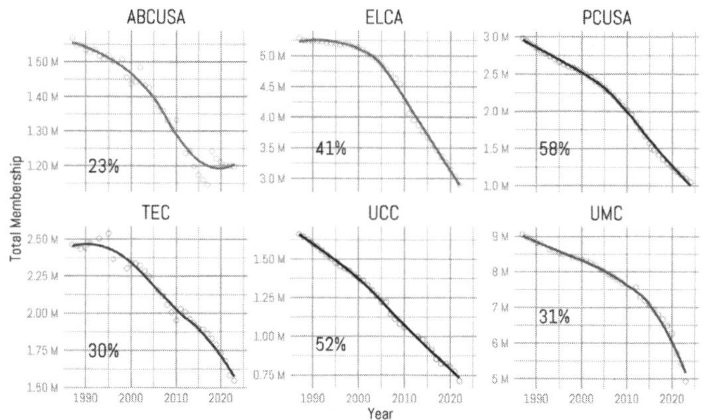

Source: @ryanburge. Data: Denominational Records

Where Do We Go from Here?

Church folk still hold out hope that Christianity's steep decline will eventually reverse or at least slow down. The Pew Research Center produced a February 2025 report titled, "Decline of Christianity in the U.S. Has Slowed, May Have Leveled Off."[20] *The New York Times* and other news outlets scooped it up, and at least a dozen friends and family who knew about my research forwarded the piece to me. Some just wanted to make sure I saw the data. Others hinted, "Maybe things aren't so bad?"

Ryan Burge posed the same question this spring, after studying figures from the newly released 2024 Cooperative Election Study. Conducted alongside presidential elections, this mammoth study gathers details from 60,000 Americans, which makes it the largest longitudinal data set available. Burge's conclusion: At least for now, the rise of the Nones is over.[21] The Nones (people who identify as "atheist," "agnostic," or "nothing in particular") grew steadily from 2008 until 2021, as their share of the American public rose from 21 percent to peak at 36 percent. Over the next three years, they essentially held at that level. Last year, Nones dropped to 34 percent.

Is the wilderness sojourn over? Have we turned a corner, and now it's time to look toward religious revival? The answer, especially for mainline Protestants, is no. There might be a short-term pause in the decline; every multi-decade graph includes some stable periods. We're also just climbing out of the pandemic trough. But the current plateau is mainly due to gains among more conservative churches and also those aligned with White Christo-nationalism, including a slight surge in Gen Z participation in Catholic and Pentecostal churches.[22]

Even these relatively positive trendlines may not last long. Why am I so certain? For the same reason the Pew Research team cited [their bold print]: "**But, despite these signs of recent stabilization and abiding spirituality, other indicators suggest we may see further declines in the American religious**

FIGURE 4

Religious Composition of Each Generation in 2024

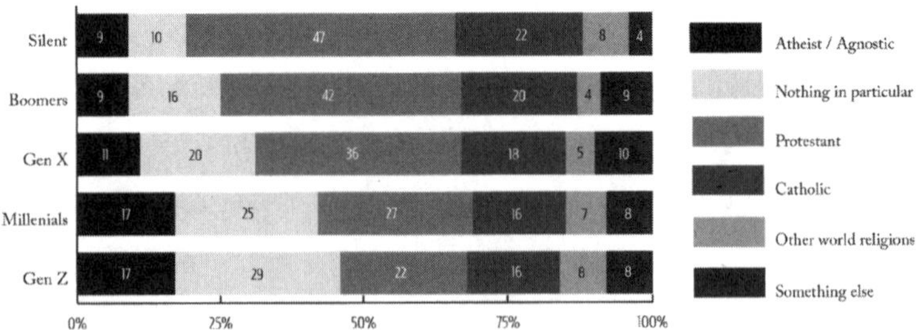

Source: @ryanburge. Data: Cooperative Election Study, 2024

landscape in future years. Namely, younger Americans remain far less religious than older adults."

Burge notes the same sobering reality in data from the Cooperative Election Study.[23] (See Figure 4.) Basically, the proportion of Nones (the "Atheist/Agnostic" and "Nothing in Particular" blocks on the left) rises consistently with each generation: Silent Generation, 19 percent; Boomers, 25 percent; Generation X, 31 percent; Millennials, 42 percent; Generation Z, 46 percent. As older Americans become less engaged and eventually pass away, the people coming behind them are less and less religious.

The Pew Center offers even more disturbing news for churches. Within each age cohort, Americans tend to become less conventionally religious and more religiously unaffiliated as they get *older* (though some have become more prayerful).[24] That's the opposite of conventional wisdom, which assumes people will get more religious and attend church more often with age and as they retire. Though there will always be some people who embrace organized religion as they go through life transitions, and recent trends I just noted suggest some Gen Z may be reconsidering religion, there is absolutely no reason to think today's Millennials and Gen Zers will *en masse* embrace organized religion and pull churches from the valley.

What about conversion, or what researchers call "switching"? It happens, but Christianity consistently loses more people to nonreligion than it gains. Pew researchers sum up the dim prospects with this simple statement: "For every person who was raised as a 'None' and now identifies with a religion, 5.9 people have switched away from their childhood religion and no longer identify with any religion."[25]

The State of the Nones

The next chapter takes an unflinching look at why and how disaffiliation has risen so rapidly and steadily in America—essentially, exploring the cultural forces that have fostered the boom among Nones and Dones. Before we shift to that conversation, I want to share a bit more about who the Nones are . . . and who they are not.

Nones Are Multicultural

Religious disaffiliation is firmly established across racial lines. Check out the percentage of each racial group who identify as Nones.[26]

- Black: 22 percent
- Hispanic: 27 percent
- White: 31 percent
- Asian: 33 percent

These figures may be surprising considering the degree to which Black and Latino communities have historically leaned heavily on religious organizations. For Black folk, church was often the only institution where we could exercise leadership, teach the truth, and grow political power; for Latinos, churches have been a haven for preserving language and culture in an often hostile nation. Still, today Nones comprise a healthy cohort in every racial group.

> *"Christianity was used to control, especially in my household. So once I got away for school, it was very liberating to not participate in Christianity."*
>
> —E., 20, Northfield, MN

Nones Are Evenly Split by Gender

While men make up a slight majority of the Nones overall (51 percent male versus 47 percent female),[27] that gender gap is closing among younger Nones. Today 54 percent of Gen Zers who've left religion are women, whereas men dominate in every other generation.[28]

Nones Are More Liberal

The liberal exodus from Christianity has been tagged as one of the drivers around the rise of Nones (you'll hear more about why in the next chapter). More than seven in ten Nones identify as Democrats or lean toward the Democratic Party.[29] A note: Christians overall tend to favor the Republican Party (6 in 10 Protestants and a little more than half of Catholics).

Nones Are Mixed on Education

Among Nones, a little more than a third are college graduates, a little less than a third have some college under their belt, and a solid third stopped with a high school education.[30] So Nones are by no means the intellectual elite.

If anything, as Ryan Burge discovered when he crunched the Cooperative Election Study figures, it appears a higher level of education correlates with a greater likelihood of regular church attendance.[31] Only 18 percent of people who haven't completed high school say they attend church weekly. On the other end of the scale, 27 percent of people with a four-year college degree are regulars, and 30 percent of those who've done post-grad work attend worship every week.

Nones and Religion

The cohort of Nones includes a stable group of people who identify as atheist and agnostic; the percentage of atheists and agnostics in America hasn't changed much in the last twenty years. By far, the greatest proportion of Nones say they are "Nothing in particular," a broad category that encompasses everyone from the conflicted Christian who still shows up in the pews, to the spiritually vibrant person who eschews labels, to the ambivalent person who genuinely doesn't care about religion at all.[32]

FIGURE 5

Religious Identification of Nones

Percentage of Nones who say they are ...

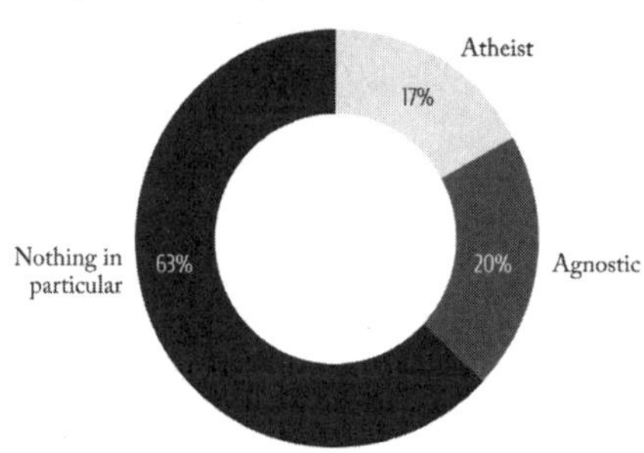

Source: Pew Research Center, 2023

Indeed, studies consistently report that Nones can be quite spiritual (by some measures, many are even religious, though they eschew the label). Nearly half of Nones say they are spiritual or that spirituality is important to them. The Pew Center has tracked religious beliefs and practices among Nones and compared them with religiously affiliated people.[33] Figures 6 and 7 describe how the two groups stack up.

FIGURES 6 AND 7:

Religious Beliefs of Nones vs. Religiously Affiliated Adults

Percentages of each group who say they...

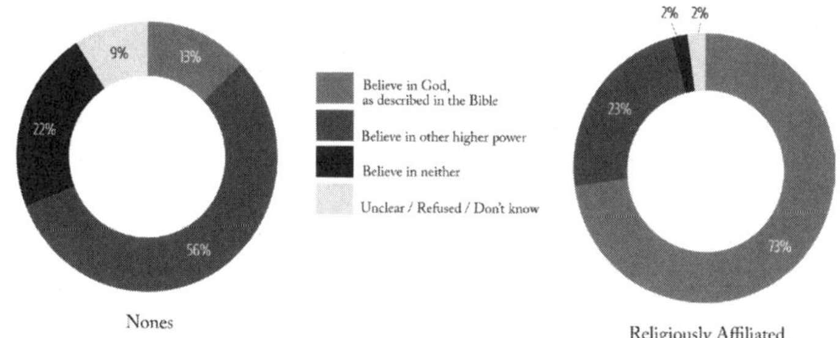

Source: Pew Research Center, 2023

Religious Practices of Nones vs. Religiously Affiliated Adults

Percentages of each group who say they...

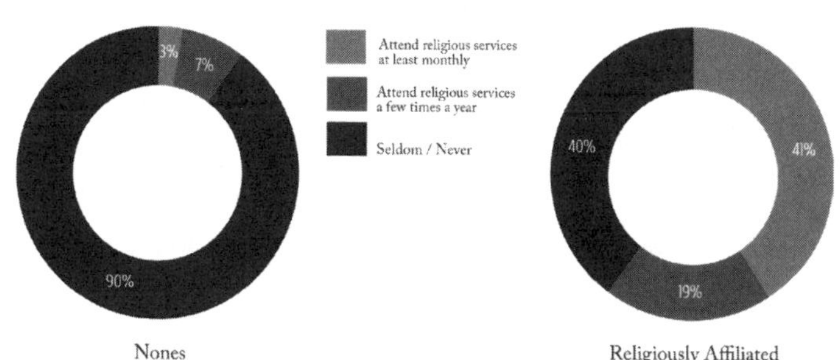

Source: Pew Research Center, 2023

As the data above makes clear, not all Nones are atheists. Most believe in a higher power, and some even believe in the God described in the Bible. The vast majority don't go to church, but 10 percent attend anywhere from a few times a year to once a month or even once a week. In other words, a lot of people in the pews are also Nones who've chosen not to formally claim to be Christian (I certainly found this to be true among my conversation partners and even among members of the Episcopal church where I serve).

What drove so many people to say no to religion? Later, we will hear story after story from my conversation partners. Across America, certain factors rise to the top. Some 60 percent say they question religious teachings, 47 percent don't like religious organizations, and 41 percent don't see a need for religion in their lives. Smaller proportions say they don't believe in God or a higher power (32 percent), had bad experiences with religious people (30 percent), or just don't have time for religion (12 percent).[34]

Americans Still Believe in God

If you need some good news, keep in mind that, even as religious affiliation has diminished significantly across the board, overall belief and practice (at least the practice of prayer) have proved quite durable.[35]

- 86 percent believe people have a soul or spirit in addition to their physical body.
- 83 percent believe in God or a universal spirit.
- 79 percent believe there is something spiritual beyond the natural world, even if we can't see it.
- 70 percent believe in an afterlife (heaven, hell, or both).
- 44 percent pray at least once a day.

Americans are holding onto a belief in God and the spirit realm, and many of them still pause at least once a day for prayer of some kind. They just don't think church membership or explicit adherence to a particular religion is necessary.

—//—

Given the history, patterns, and figures we've now explored, no one can deny America is becoming a less and less traditionally Christian nation. It helps to remember that mainline Protestantism's rousing success in the 1950s and 1960s—while definitive for many of the elders who still anchor today's churches—was something of an aberration. We only developed that overt faithfulness after the turmoil of two wars and a determined civic, religious, and political effort to redefine, rebuild, and protect a growing nation.

It's also encouraging to note how strongly religious freedom and spiritual vitality have always coursed through the nation's lifeblood. Our compass keeps pointing to the holy, even as the pathways get more diverse. That is certainly the case in today's pluralistic, increasingly post-Christian landscape, as we will see in the next chapter.

Where Did Everybody Go?:

Why the Pews Emptied and the Nones Grew

Fifty years ago, 90 percent of Americans identified as Christian. But people born in this century are more likely to claim no religion at all. What happened? How did we become a nation where successive generations have so little interest in the faith that once anchored . . . well . . . everything?

Plenty of the church's wounds are self-inflicted. The list of Christian failures grows longer with each day: clergy sex scandals, financial abuse, White Christo-nationalism, homophobia and transphobia, hypocrisy, and so many more betrayals of the way of Jesus. But those horrors aren't exactly new. The scale and speed of overall change from religiously affiliated to unaffiliated suggests there's more at work here than a severe reaction to the ills of the church. Let's study the cultural factors that have depressed religious and civic participation, and how those same factors have nurtured fertile ground for Nones to rise up strong.

The Dropped Baton

Of all the explanations for accelerating disaffiliation from Christianity, the most meaningful may also be the simplest: Church-going generations are passing away, and they aren't being replaced by emerging generations. Researchers call this "generational replacement," and it's technically the number-one driver behind Christianity's fall-off and the growth of Nones and Dones.

We've already seen some of the evidence, including this data from our friend Ryan Burge.[1]

FIGURE 4

Religious Composition of Each Generation in 2024

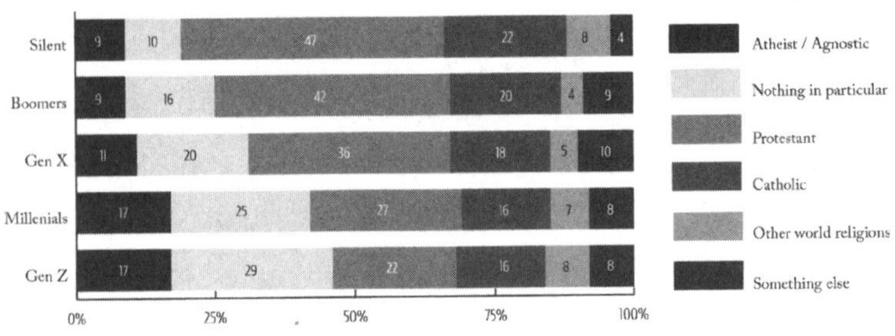

Source: @ryanburge. Data: Cooperative Election Study, 2024

Imagine the rows above are on a scroll. Eventually, the Silent Generation's strong religious participation will roll away, and the Boomers will be at the top, less religious than their departed neighbors but more active than Gen X and younger groups just below on the scroll. Now pay attention to the bottom of the graph. You can't see them yet, but soon the group tentatively called "Gen Alpha" will appear, likely with religious sensibilities closer to Gen Z than their older, more religious fellow Americans.

Again, we should keep asking why. There are a few reasons, and they tend to cluster around the family:

1. One indicator of current religious identity and participation is your family of origin's religiosity. Younger generations are less likely to report that they were raised in religious households than older generations.[2] For instance, about 17 percent of Millennials said they were not raised in any particular religion. Only 5 percent of Baby Boomers said the same.[3]
2. Another indicator is weekly or regular worship attendance growing up. About one in three Millennials say they attended weekly religious services with their family when they were young. Compare that to Baby Boomers, half of whom worshiped weekly as children.[4]
3. Formal religious education is also a strong indicator of current religiosity. In the Pew Center research, 42 percent of people in the youngest age group (18–24) said they received no formal religious education at all, compared to only 20 percent of the oldest age group (74+).

"Mom took us to a Methodist church, and my dad always stayed home. At a certain point, she asked, 'Do you want to go?' It never really connected for me."

—E., 32, Atlanta

If you think of faith as a generational relay race, the Baby Boomers received the faith baton from their parents, but a significant group of them rebelled against those structures and instead explored alternative spiritual pathways or none at all. That cohort chose to raise their children (the bulk of whom are Millennials) with greater freedom and less structure around faith identity, regular worship or religious education. Generation X started out with a little less religious background than their Boomer predecessors, and when they raised their children (largely Gen Z), they opted for more freedom, too. Again, it's tough to imagine that Millennials—only 43 percent of whom identify as Christian—will suddenly swing toward greater religious engagement and education for their children.

The baton of faith simply hasn't been passed along. In the absence of that steady transmission of Christian faith and practice from one cohort to the next, generational replacement breaks down, and the numbers tank. But why did those Boomer and Gen X parents opt out of religion? Why are even members of the Silent Generation more likely to identify as Nones in their later years? What's happening in the soil, such that traditional religion doesn't flourish like it used to but Nones proliferate?

From the Age of Mobilization to the Age of Authenticity

In his epic *A Secular Age*, philosopher Charles Taylor explains how the West has shifted from a culture of community and association to one marked by individual freedom and the quest for authenticity. During what he calls the Age of Mobilization[5]—which shaped the Western world from 1800 to 1960—people tended to derive identity, truth, and authority from institutions and group associations. Many of those ties broke down in the 1960s. Taylor says new generations dismissed the Age of Mobilization "[as] conformist, crushing individuality and creativity, as too concerned with production and concrete results, as repressing feeling and spontaneity, as exalting the mechanical over the organic."[6]

In its place rose the Age of Authenticity and "expressive individualism." Even if you don't know the term, you'll recognize phrases like, "You be you," "Be true to yourself," and "Follow your heart." Basically, expressive individualism asserts the highest entity is the self, and your highest work is to discover, express, and actualize your genuine, true, *authentic* self. Anything that forces you to conform or to be inauthentic—especially external authorities and institutions—should be cast aside in favor of your personal experience and inner wisdom.[7]

Needless to say, traditional, organized religion and civic institutions all suffer in this milieu. As Taylor explains, "the religious life or practice that I become part of must not only be my choice, but it must speak to me, it must make sense in terms of my spiritual development as I understand this."[8] If that's your mindset, you'll probably favor the infinitely customizable pathway of the Nones and spiritual but not religious and abandon declining religious institutions.

Is Religion Obsolete?

Sociologist of religion Christian Smith goes a step further and makes the compelling argument that traditional religion isn't just declining. He wonders if it has become culturally obsolete.

A note: When Smith speaks of traditional religion, he's talking about all the mainline Protestant denominations, plus the Roman Catholics and evangelicals, as well as Jewish and Muslim faith communities.[9] How do such bedrock institutions go obsolete? Smith says it's quite simple:

> Something becomes obsolete when most people feel it is no longer useful or needed because something else has superseded it in function, efficiency, value, or interest. Obsolete connotes outdated or old-fashioned, in the sense of being "put out of business" or style by some innovation, incompatible larger trend, or perceived change in functional need.[10]

Smith's point immediately resonated for me. As a young person, I loved my personal Selectric typewriter. My mom was an administrative assistant, so having my own typewriter by age twelve was a sign I had grown up. The machine brought me such joy: the click and clack of lettered hammers hitting paper, the thwack of the returning carriage. I even loved the tiny bottle of White-Out near my right hand, because everybody makes mistakes. But when the desktop computer came along, I couldn't make the case for my beloved Selectric anymore.

Now, I can't even remember the desktop; most everything I watch, compose, or calculate is on either a laptop, iPad, or cell phone (granted I revert to paper, pen, and colored pencils when I need to spark creativity or talk to God). The typewriter doesn't make sense in my world. It doesn't perform the functions I need it to, not like other devices that I now prefer to use. And while seeing a typewriter might inspire fond memories, and I bear no ill will toward the machine, I wouldn't dream of actually using one now.

According to Smith, that's how a growing proportion of Americans feel about traditional religion. Even if they are interested in spirituality, organized religions simply don't cross their minds. It's certainly what I heard from my Millennial and Gen Z conversation partners across America.

> *"Some people are more vehemently anti-religion. I don't really care. You just do whatever you want. I'll do whatever I want."*
>
> —J., 25, Claremont, CA

In addition to the notion of obsolescence, Smith speaks eloquently of the "cultural mismatch" between traditional religion and contemporary culture. Organized faith evokes a particular mood, one rooted in institutional trust, books, top-down leadership, historic ties, physical place, community, and stability. Smith says Millennials and Gen Zers find such things "archaic, clunky, overbearing, weird, and frustrating."[11] Ouch.

Now stand all that tradition up next to contemporary culture, or what Smith refers to as the "Millennial zeitgeist."[ii] A zeitgeist isn't necessarily everyone's identity or experience, but it is a prevailing tenor for a time. Think of the Roaring Twenties or the Sixties Counterculture. Smith describes these marks of the Millennial zeitgeist:[12]

- *Individualistic*: Envisioning society as a collection of atomistic, choice-making selves
- *Anti-institutional*: Avoiding structured social groups and institutions
- *Relativist*: Viewing knowledge, truth, and ethics as opinions dependent on perspectives
- *Subjectivist*: Assuming interior feelings and experience to be the best guides for living

---

ii The *Oxford English Dictionary* says a zeitgeist is a "defining mood or mood of a particular period of history as shown by the ideas and beliefs of the time." https://www.oed.com.

- *Anti-authority*: Hostile to structured social roles of influence and power
- *Fluid*: Expecting change, instability, revision, mobility
- *Multicultural*: Comfortable with sociocultural diversity, dubious of homogenous groups

A very important clarification: This zeitgeist is not Millennial because it's associated with Millennials; it's Millennial because it solidified around the turn of the millennium. The truth is, the Baby Boomers planted these seeds—promotion of individual freedom, distrust of institutions, reliance on technology and market culture—in the 1960s and 1970s. Other forces have combined to make the Millennial zeitgeist the defining mood within which most younger adults have always existed. That spells doom for traditional faith. Or as Smith concludes: "Religion in the Millennial zeitgeist felt alien and disconnected from what mattered in life—in short, badly culturally mismatched. The vibes were off."[13]

Prime Cultural Movers

All this still begs the question: Why? Why have the Age of Authenticity and the Millennial zeitgeist formed in this way at this time? Why have individualism, anti-institutionalism, relativism, fluidity, and multiculturalism flourished to such a degree over the last fifty years? What are the forces and currents shaping our contemporary, post-Christian milieu? I'd like to add more voices to the conversation and contribute my own thoughts about American religious and nonreligious life today.

Privatization

Socio-cultural scholars James Emery White and Peter Berger agree there are three currents propelling American culture beyond Christianity: privatization, secularization, and pluralization. The most potent of those forces may be privatization, which White says creates a chasm "between the public and the private spheres of life, and spiritual things are increasingly placed within the private arena."[14] Privatization takes religion and spirituality—systems which are intended to shape entire worlds, touch all parts of our existence, and fill every corner with meaning—and instead makes them small, individual, quiet matters of personal preference. Privatization isolates faith and isolates us, until the self is the only source of truth and authority we can trust.

Nothing has privatized American life, walled us off from civic and religious community, and tucked us into individual, self-autonomous pods quite like modern technology. The automobile, television, internet, and mobile phone: Each has delivered enormous gains in productivity, connectivity, and mobility. We know more about everything and can go most anywhere, and we are less connected to one another and to the God who shows up where two or more are gathered.

The Amish of southeastern Pennsylvania understood this danger instinctively. An ethnographer once asked about their process of discerning what technologies to admit and which to refuse. They shared this nugget of wisdom:

> We can almost always tell if a change will bring good or bad tidings. Certain things we definitely do not want, like the television and the radio. They would destroy our visiting practices. We

> would stay at home with the television or radio rather than meet with other people. The visiting practices are important because of the closeness of the people. How can we care for the neighbor if we do not visit them or know what is going on in their lives?[15]

The Amish immediately recognized the tempting lure of the glowing box in the center of the room. Indeed, between 1965 and 1995, Americans gained an average of six hours a week in additional free time. Where did we spend it? Not reading or cooking or pursuing personal hobbies. Not visiting friends. Not volunteering in the community. Not playing with our children. We spent most all of those extra hours in front of the TV.[16]

Who could blame us? Seeing beloved characters on-screen can stir the same emotions as interacting with actual people you know. That's not only in our heads. Scientists now understand that watching your favorite television shows delivers hits of dopamine, the "feel-good hormone,"[17] a neurotransmitter linked to bliss and euphoria. They report binge-watching a series can produce a "drug-like high,"[18] leaving us chasing the next bump of comfort and joy, helpless to resist or to reduce our consumption.

> *"A lot of us want community, but we don't know where to find it. Everyone has access to almost everything they need or want directly on their phone. Everything but connecting to another person in-person."*
>
> —V., 30, San Francisco

When Apple introduced the iPhone in 2007, they placed the whole of the internet and all its temptations in our back pockets, in the palm of our hands, and on the nightstand, where it's the last thing we see before sleeping and the first thing we touch upon waking. According to Christian Smith's

2023 Millennial Zeitgeist Survey, Millennials spend roughly five hours a day online, not counting work. Gen Xers clocked in at 3.7 hours; Later Boomers, three hours; Early Boomers, 3.3 hours.[19] We only have twenty-four hours in a day, so that's time we're not spending with one another.

Worse still, the abundance of time alone and on-screen is rewiring our brains. After a period watching TV, surfing the web, or scrolling TikTok alone, when the dopamine wears off, we don't feel refreshed or ready to connect with others. Instead, we crave more "me" time. Brené Brown explains it this way:

> When we feel isolated, disconnected, and lonely, we try to protect ourselves. In that mode, we want to connect, but our brain is attempting to override connection with self-protection. That means less empathy, more defensiveness, more numbing, and less sleeping . . . Unchecked loneliness fuels continued loneliness by keeping us afraid to reach out.[20]

Brown raised the "L" word, and she's not the only one talking about it. Former U.S. Surgeon General Vivek Murthy made headlines in 2023 when he declared loneliness an epidemic as dangerous as smoking and obesity.[21] Apparently, instead of emerging from lockdown and rebuilding connections, Americans overall spent *more* time alone in 2023 than we did in 2021.[22]

In "The Antisocial Century," Derek Thompson traces America's movement from being alone to being lonely to being downright antisocial. Thompson cites the work of Patrick Sharkey, who says we have become "more likely to take meetings from home, to shop from home, to be entertained at home, to eat at home, and even to worship at home. Practically the entire economy has reoriented itself to allow Americans to stay within their four walls. This phenomenon cannot be reduced to remote work. It is something far more totalizing—something more like 'remote life.'"[23]

It's hard to see where religious life fits into this privatized pod, when it's so much easier to eat, work, read, practice, and pursue spirituality at a distance from other people.

Secularization

The next current pushing us away from traditional religion is secularization, which Peter Berger defines as the process of moving sectors of society and culture out "from the domination of religious institutions and symbols."[24] If the goal of religion is to establish a sacred cosmos within which everything has a meaning and order, secularization aims to peel religious symbols, words, structures, and meaning systems away from the social order.

Judging by the number of Americans who still claim a belief in God or a higher power, believe we have souls, pray at least once a day, and seek the spirit in nature, we are far from a fully secular nation. That doesn't mean secularization—a reduction in the "*domination* of religious institutions and symbols" [my italics]—is not happening. Religion is undoubtedly a less dominant and defining force over the culture. Here is the proof:

First, notice the very emergence of the Nones. There have always been people who didn't agree with religion or accept faith-based meaning systems. But in 1956, when 96 percent of Americans said they were Christian, or even in 1971, when 90 percent affiliated with Christianity, the social pressures supporting religious affiliation were too strong for most people to feel safe about public defiance. What looks like a boom in the number of Nones may in part be people across generations finally speaking their truth, now that religion holds less sway over the wider culture or their lives.

I would also argue that secularization explains another interesting and unfortunate trend in religious participation: the disappearance of progressive Christians.

Mainline Protestant denominations have been vexed at our membership troubles over the last thirty years. People criticize Christianity for its misogyny, racism, and general support of conservative policies. So why don't they flock to more inclusive and social justice-oriented churches? Where are the liberal Christians?

In fact, well into the 1980s, Democrats and Republicans were both about 87 percent Christian, and mainline decline was fairly modest.[25] The slippage began in the 1990s, just as the Religious Right emerged as a force in American life and politics. As a result, Michael Hout and Claude Fischer maintain, "liberals and young people who already had weak attachment to organized religion [tended] to drop that identification."[26] Before long, liberal and even moderate Americans began to shed association with Christianity, even though they had positive experiences in their home churches (my interviews with young adult Nones and Dones certainly affirm this point). That effect has only accelerated since the election of President Donald Trump in both 2016 and 2024, each time with a majority of the White Christian vote. A critical mass of scholars now argue that negative associations between faith and political conservatism

"Our decision to step away from what was becoming a pretty conservative church was intentional. Even having the conversation with my parents was weird, telling them, 'It's not that we don't believe in God anymore. But we are leaving the church.'"

—J., 41, Atlanta

have driven scores of liberal Americans to disaffiliate from Christianity.[27]

Jay Demerath points to another reason why mainline Protestant churches tanked at the very same time America became more progressive. As we scored wins around gender, racial, and economic justice, social justice-identified churches became less necessary or distinctive. Why go to church if it sounds just like the wider culture? On the other hand, conservative churches remained vital to the Religious Right's uphill culture battle. Conservative, evangelical Christianity got stronger, while the mainline grew weak.[28]

Add up all these factors, and it's no wonder Pew researchers found that only 37 percent of ideological liberals identified as Christian in 2024, down from 62 percent in 2007. Meanwhile, the majority of liberal Americans are now Nones; in 2024, 51 percent of liberals said they have *no* religion, up from 27 percent in 2007.[29] These former Christians no longer care for spaces or institutions allied with Christianity, largely because the Christianity they see in public opposes the values they hold most dear.

While they may still believe in God, pray regularly, maintain private expressions of faith, and even attend church occasionally, Christian religion does not control or shape their lives and cultures as it once did. In other words, they are becoming more secular and less religious.

Pluralization

This brings us to the final current assisting the flow of people away from organized religion and toward no affiliation at all: pluralization, which White says presents us with "a staggering number of ideologies and faith options competing for their attention."[30]

On the whole, pluralization is a good. Thanks to the constitutional guarantee of religious freedom, America has long provided fertile soil where myriad religious flowers could bloom. Students of secularism have often wondered why the United States isn't as secular as our industrialized, European peers. Apparently, when there's no state church enforcing uniformity, people have less to reject and react against and feel free to explore and experiment, revive and reform.

As different cultural and racial groups have migrated to America, they've added fresh spiritual and philosophical perspectives to this already colorful mix. On one hand, it means we have more opportunities to navigate and even celebrate difference. It also means people who don't resonate with the tradition of their childhood or community can inquire into other pathways to the divine. I don't know where I would be if I hadn't discovered Buddhism and Hinduism in college. Even if I'm now a Christian, I haven't felt the need to disavow the gifts of those traditions, many of which are complementary and beneficial to Christian life.

On the other hand, if you imagine the nation as a spiritual marketplace, these more recent arrivals have stocked entire new sections of the store. Shoppers can pick and choose, mix and match, try something out and then bring it back for a refund if it doesn't satisfy their appetite. Such free borrowing raises real questions about whether the borrowers respect the integrity and history of the tradition or the group that birthed it. There is

> *"Sometimes I wonder if my inability to commit is because the internet creates the sense that there are infinite options. Even if I pick a path, I always wonder if there's a better option out there."*
>
> —A., 31, Atlanta

also a good chance that once I've crafted my perfect mixture, I won't find anyone else who shares it. They've all got their own bespoke spiritual bento box, too.

This pluralizing approach shapes far more than religious life in America. Especially thanks to the internet, we have infinite access to infinite possibilities and infinite choice in almost every part of life. Few humans can process that volume of information without freezing up or spinning out. As a result, my conversation partners told me pluralization can make it tough to focus attention or to choose anything, including a life partner, a home, or a spiritual path.

Now combine the effect of privatization (which places us in small pods where we become the highest authorities over and experts on our own existence) and secularization (which reduces the power of wider traditions and even God over our lives). Would you like to experiment with body customization and then preview the brand-new you, available for purchase? There's an app for that. Maybe you'd like to create a customized spiritual path, drawing on a global repository of cultural and spiritual wisdom to assemble your own personal set of practices, readings, and meaning-making strategies . . . all freed from the complications of consistency, history, or commitment to other people. There's an app for that.

—//—

Where do these movements and forces leave Christianity? In exactly the place we find ourselves now. For better or worse, once you eliminate the uniqueness of the Christian message as an expression of divine truth, and once you've swept aside the promise of heaven and the threat of eternal damnation, and once the social rewards of church association have disappeared because fewer people attend, and once it's difficult to publicly identify with Christianity and still be considered kind or intelligent or inclusive, and once you've pushed faith into a small private enclave that's best not exposed in public, and once you allow each of us to fill that niche with all that our hearts desire via a handheld device, well . . . you don't need artificial intelligence to predict further disaffiliation and decline on the horizon.

That conflict is especially keen for mainline Protestant, establishment churches who have traditionally aligned with the prevailing culture. When that culture is the Millennial zeitgeist (which values individual freedom, privatization, relativism, fluidity, and inclusivity and tends to question authority), you can see how a culturally "relevant" church that tells people to go where they want, believe what they want, and hold commitment lightly could unintentionally run itself out of business.

The Age of Authenticity might prove unfriendly for traditional religion, but it's no picnic for Nones and Dones, either. Privatization encourages the individual pursuit of your authentic self apart from institutions and external authorities, but it can be a desperately lonely path. Secularization carves out more spaces where being nonreligious or unaffiliated is acceptable and even expected, but what if you yearn for the ancient, the beautiful, and the holy? Pluralization gives you infinite access and permission to harness a world of resources so you can construct your best life, but will anything ever feel like home?

Those are just some of the questions I've heard Millennial and Gen Z Nones and Dones asking as they seek spiritual life and meaning. In Part II, you'll see them describe how and where they encounter the sacred, community, and belonging; what they're creating; and what barriers they're encountering. Their questions and challenges may also help the church to reclaim our identity as followers of Jesus animated by his Holy Spirit, and not as mere purveyors of culture. For an increasingly obsolete church, partnerships like this may be the only viable path to life.

THE NONES AND DONES SPEAK

In the chapters that follow, we will open the gallery and hear more about the spiritual lives, communities, and witness of Millennial and Gen Z Nones and Dones living in the post-Christian, Millennial zeitgeist. Before sharing those stories, I should explain how an Episcopal priest ended up meeting and having deep conversations with forty-five younger, nonreligious people, most of them strangers with an ingrained distrust for religion and authority.

Locations

I began by identifying four metro areas for the interviews: San Francisco Bay area (West Coast), Minnesota's Twin Cities (Midwest), metro Atlanta (South) and New York (Northeast). I supplemented with a trip to Northfield, Minnesota (a college town with strong farming ties) and Zoom interviews with people in Clarksville, Tennessee; Cambridge, Massachusetts; and Philadelphia, Pennsylvania. I would have appreciated widening the sample by traveling further afield, especially to smaller towns and rural areas, but budget and time constraints didn't make that broader survey possible. I also prioritized in-person interviews rather than conducting more Zoom interviews across more locations.

Comparing my results with studies that covered a wider geographic range,[1] I feel confident that the same sociocultural factors we heard about in Chapter 2—the shift from the Age of Mobilization to the Age of Authenticity, the emergence of expressive individualism, the development of the Millennial zeitgeist, plus privatization, secularization, and pluralization—all apply to varying degrees across urban, suburban, and rural areas.

Recruitment

I posted on Facebook and Instagram in November and December 2024 and January 2025, asking more than seven thousand contacts to help me to identify nonreligious people ages 18–44 in the four locations described above for a conversation about their spiritual journeys, experiences of the sacred and community, and what wisdom they would offer to churches. Some contacts got excited, activated their own networks, and identified people I could interview. I also specifically invited young adults who once attended the church I serve in New York; two of them are part of the sample.

Demographic Sensitivity

Millennials and Gen Zers tend to be a more racially diverse group than the population at large. With some extra effort, I was able to gather a wide range of racial and cultural voices (please note that biracial people are counted partially in each of the racial groups with which they identified, rather than sorting them all into a separate "mixed race" category):

- Asian: 5.5
- Black: 8.5
- Indigenous: 1
- Latino: 7
- White: 23

I did not inquire specifically about sexual orientation or political affiliation, although people were very comfortable sharing and both components of identity often figured highly in their spiritual journeys. I should note that my study group skews toward liberal, which tracks with the overall tendency of Nones (as of 2023, 70 percent of Nones align with the Democratic Party or lean that direction),[2] as well as Millennials and Gen Z (Americans in their twenties are about 65 percent Democratic-leaning).[3]

The Conversations

Most of the conversations were one-on-one sessions lasting forty-five minutes to one hour. We connected in cafes or in public meeting spaces, and in a few cases, in their homes. Each conversation centered on four prompts:

1. Tell me about your spiritual journey, from childhood to this point.
2. How and where do you experience or connect with the sacred (depending on the partner's affinity, I also asked how they experience the Ultimate, the divine, the holy, God, meaning, and mystery)?
3. How and where do you experience community and belonging?
4. What would you tell the church/organized religion, if it was really listening? (Again, depending on how people responded to this open question, I sometimes went on to add: "What do you wish churches understood better, especially if they want to understand you, your generation, the

culture you inhabit, and the challenges you face?" or "What are churches missing about life and spirituality today?")

For help conducting similar conversations with Nones and Dones, see the reflection guide at www.stephaniespellers.com/church-tomorrow.

Whenever possible, I sent my partners the questions in advance, though I encouraged them not to write or perfect their answers ahead of time. They were all informed that I am an Episcopal clergy person, though I did not wear my collar or other clerical garb when we met. I made clear in every interview that I had no ulterior motives—I wasn't trying to convince them they should believe anything or that they should attend any church. This reassurance appears to have helped to create the safe space people needed in order to share perspectives many said they had never voiced out loud.

When we met, the focus was on my partners. While I call these conversations, and I shared about my own journey or thoughts when it seemed appropriate and not likely to steer their response, the point was to hear Nones and Dones's stories and insights.

Two other important notes about the conversations and offerings that follow:

- Some peer-reviewed, larger-scale studies have used pseudonyms and others real names. I invited each participant to tell me how they wanted to be identified. What follows is therefore a mixture of real and chosen names. As a former newspaper reporter, I am used to accurately identifying sources, but I determined this project's authenticity did not hinge on those details.

- I recorded every conversation and then sent them to a high-quality AI transcription service. I also returned to partners any time I had questions and provided copies of quotes to anyone who asked.

Reading their words, I have been awed by my conversation partners' eagerness, openness, intelligence, and spiritual depth. They had clearly invested lots of thought, energy, and heart into their spiritual lives and communities, but they didn't have many outlets for talking about it. They were amazed a church person wanted to hear from them and that other church folk might eventually consider what they shared. Conversations that were scheduled for one hour sometimes stretched to ninety minutes. People texted and sent me voice notes with additional thoughts. A few asked for prayer or a blessing at the end of the interview. The hunger for spiritual, meaningful conversation and companionship was palpable, including among atheists and agnostics. I am 100 percent convinced that ample opportunities for partnership and new life await if you're willing to go forth and listen to the Nones and Dones in your life with curiosity, humility, mutuality, and love.

It was a blessing for me to meet and be so generously received by these Nones and Dones. The only thing better is now welcoming you as another partner in the conversation.

CHAPTER 3

Becoming None and Done

Question 1: Share about your spiritual journey and what led to where you are now.

Kimberley comes from a long line of Black women who took their spiritual journey into their own hands. She is forty-one and grew up in rural Maryland, where both sides of her family have been United Methodist for several generations. She's proud of her mom, who pastors a small, vibrant church, but the story that really makes her shine is about her grandmother. "My dad's family went to a Black United Methodist church in this very small town," she explained. "Well, his mom had some disagreements with the church's leadership, and she picked up and started going to the White United Methodist church."

Her grandmother's family members were livid, and she had plenty of struggles with White folks, but she stood her ground. "I just love that story about my grandmother, who died before I was born, being this pioneer. Whatever her values were that didn't align, she said, 'I'm through with y'all. This is not what I want for my spiritual experience. I'm going over there.'"

Many years later, Kimberley had to make hard choices about her own spiritual journey. She loved church as a child but drifted away in her college years. When she tried to return as an adult, she landed at an African Methodist Episcopal (AME) megachurch, but a scandal involving their popular pastor drove her back out the door.

She tried a few other churches but eventually settled into a period of wilderness wandering. While working in admissions at a private girls' school, she met a school chaplain who reopened her mind to spirituality. She left that job to train to become an interfaith hospital chaplain.

"My call was to people that did not feel a sense of belonging or didn't feel they fit within a traditional church or worship setting," she said. "I also had a longing toward people who had religious trauma or were searching for God or felt a connection to God, but weren't quite sure how to make more of it. That's also when I embraced this idea of spiritual-but-not-religious for myself."

Today, Kimberley serves as a chaplain at a Philadelphia hospital, where she accompanies people of all faiths and none at all. Where is her personal faith these days? Don't try to add a label because it won't stick. "What am I?" she asked. "Well, I like to say Jesus will always be my homeboy, but I don't think Jesus minds that I feel resonance when I read about the Buddha or witness the discipline of Islam. There's something about the rigidity of organized religion that doesn't feel congruent with the expansive, lived experience of Jesus."

Somehow I imagine Kimberley's grandmother would agree.

When I set out to ask religiously unaffiliated Millennials and Gen Zers about their spiritual journeys, how they experience the sacred and belonging, and what they need to tell churches, I wasn't sure what to expect. After all, most ordinary people, even the ones active in a faith community, don't have much occasion to share about the story of their life with God. Would these nonreligious people be intimidated? Try to give me the "right" answers?

I needn't have worried. Nearly every interview started or ended with something like, "Thank you for asking this." My conversation partners came to the table with such refreshing earnestness and honesty, it was like my college days sitting up with friends until three a.m. sharing deep thoughts.

This chapter focuses on their responses to the first of four prompts: "Tell me about your spiritual journey from childhood to this point." While I didn't ask anyone, "Why did you leave church?" or "How did you become a None or Done?," every narrative touched on those turning points. Each had come to the moment we heard Kimberley articulate, where they had to ask, "Do I need to be in a church?" and the answer—sometimes painful to admit, sometimes surprisingly easy—was no.

We'll open with a brief dive into a phrase that shows up in most every conversation about the spiritual lives of Nones and Dones: "spiritual but not religious." Afterward, we will explore their narratives about disaffiliating from religion, which I've organized under five headings:

- No, because I don't believe
- No, because churches hurt people

- No, because church isn't worth the trouble
- No, because I can't be labeled or pinned down
- No, because I was never religious anyway

But first, *that* phrase . . .

Being Spiritual but Not Religious

"I'm spiritual but not religious." So say millions of people who opt out of the structure, dogma, and rules of religion, but maintain their personal connection with a spiritual reality. Even if the exact phrase isn't on every None's tongue, the words came up so often, I stopped trying to find a fresh way of articulating what I was hearing. With a few important exceptions, the Millennial and Gen Z Nones and Dones with whom I spoke see themselves on a decidedly spiritual-but-not-religious (or at least not religiously affiliated) journey.

What do the words even mean to them? Spiritual, for many of my conversation partners, is concerned with a more unmediated, personal, and experiential connection with the divine, the ultimate, the sacred. Spiritual is the realm where we explore life's deepest meaning and pursue our true purpose. Religion, on the other hand, is anchored in history, tradition, institution, and doctrine. Religion presumes assent to and membership in a particular group with a specific set of beliefs. It can certainly facilitate spirituality, but surprisingly few of my partners could cite a moment when church or worship connected them to the sacred, even the ones who were quite positive about their church experiences.

Here's how Victor—a 30-year-old Black-White man who grew up Episcopalian—explained it to me.

> I see religion as a structured way to have faith, but you don't need religion to have faith. It just enhances it, gives you a different appreciation, but it's not required. It's a way to meet people that have similar values to you and to be in a sacred space where you can get closer to whatever you're seeking. It doesn't really matter. As long as you feel more peace, then that's the goal.

Victor discovers that peace when he's with friends, making art, and meditating. He's also surprisingly willing to periodically visit his old church in San Francisco (a relief to his dad, who is a priest).

Kelly is forty, White, married, and lives in Minneapolis, where she is studying to become an interfaith hospital chaplain. She has separated spirituality from church for most of her life. "Spirituality and loving God and church have been different things, even when I was a lot younger," she said. "Catholics talk about that experience of transcendence, the inbreaking of grace into the world. I never really experienced it in Mass."

Without realizing it, Kelly and Victor naturally picked up on the sociocultural forces we heard about in Chapter 2. Notice how they've prioritized an individual, private experience of the sacred over a corporate encounter in the context of church. There's also the secular distrust and decentering of religious institutions, traditions, and structures.

That was Andy's struggle growing up Latino and Catholic in Texas.

> I had a hard time with a ghostly authoritarian figure that's finger-wagging at me from a distance. And I really had a hard

> time with institutions and organizing. I personally had to separate the church and spirituality because the church is a man-made thing. For people who really believe in their religion, I think it's great. It helps instill good values, gives them community. But I like to think of myself as a very honest person, and I would feel like an imposter being all the way in with church.

Andy needed to be truthful in his relationship with God, and that meant he couldn't in good faith be part of a church. That's just one reason why so many Millennials and Gen Zers are choosing the religiously unaffiliated path of the Nones and Dones. Let's hear more of their stories now, grouped under five headings.

No . . . Because I Don't Believe

Several of my conversation partners were truly vexed by one question: "Do you agree with religious teachings about God and other tenets of the faith?"

Grete spent much of her life answering yes. She's forty-four, White, and grew up in a Protestant church along California's Central Coast. The congregation became more evangelical in the 1990s, and she was all in. "In high school, I became on fire for God. I did YWAM [Youth with a Mission, a global missionary program for evangelical college grads]. I even went to Fuller Seminary and studied arts and theology."

Like many former evangelicals or "exvangelicals," Grete started asking difficult questions about Scripture and deconstructing her faith, all of which made it impossible for her to remain Christian. Eventually, she recalled:

> Everything just exploded. I had this epiphany: It is a choice to believe that Jesus was literally the son of God, that this is the only way to get into heaven, even that God exists. Those are things you can choose to believe or not believe. Is it making me happier or is it bumming me out that I'm constantly judging myself and judging everyone else? I had to decide that I was not a Christian anymore.

Grete recently wrote her own book about leaving Christianity behind, partly because the process was so lonely for her. It can be painfully isolating when you're the only one you know who doesn't believe the church's teachings. And yet, across the country and across every age and racial group, lack of belief in faith doctrines is a primary reason Nones and Dones walk away from or never engage with religion.

Ashley and Dustin, both forty and White, are married and live in Clarksville, Tennessee with their 3-year-old son. Ashley, who uses they/them pronouns, vividly recalls the decision to personally step away from religion. "The short story is, when I was eight years old, I found my teeth from the Tooth Fairy," they said. "At that moment, I decided, 'Okay, it's all made up. These are all just things my mom's telling me are true.' I didn't know the difference between the Tooth Fairy and Santa and Jesus. That all felt the same."

The longer story is that Ashley's mom grew up Roman Catholic but left it behind. Raising kids in the rural South, she felt she needed to affiliate with a church, and she chose the Episcopalians. Ashley enjoyed being part of the community, but the questions about religion persisted. "At about age fourteen, I started researching religion intensely because what I was told was the truth just didn't make sense," Ashley said. "It wasn't something the adults in my life were super enthusiastic about."

Only after Ashley departed for college in South Carolina did they discover popular atheist authors like Christopher Hitchens. "I remember thinking, 'Oh, so there's like a word for people who don't believe. It's not just me.'" Ashley joined a secular student group and ended up meeting their now husband, Dustin.

Like Ashley, Dustin grew up in the rural South; his family was deeply committed to the Baptist Church in West Virginia. He tried to follow all the rules, but by 2009, the questions crept in, and he took his curiosity to Reddit. "I started reading more about different kinds of religion, different ways of expressing faith," he said. "I kept coming back to, 'None of this stuff is compatible. It's not even internally consistent. It all seems contradictory, and I can't explain why I believe this anymore.'"

He was quick to clarify his state of mind at the time. "It wasn't an anger thing or a resentment thing. It was just, 'I don't believe this.'"

Liam reached the same point as a teen in New York. His family was and is still active in The Episcopal Church, and he smiles as he recalls joining the youth group, serving as a worship assistant, and being part of the church family. "It was great. I would not trade that for anything."

What shifted for Liam, who is twenty-seven and White? "I reached that age where your preset beliefs that you've been following since childhood start to unravel," he said. "There was nothing to be against. It was just more that my beliefs drifted away. At some point in that process, I realized that I'm not really a believer in the whole concept of God."

Julia felt freedom when, like Liam, she could admit she didn't believe in religious doctrines. A Nebraska native, she's twenty-five and now lives in New York. "I remember deciding at eight or nine, I must be agnostic," she recalled. "Religion just made me really stressed as a kid. It was so overwhelming. There's so many different religions; there's no way my religion would be right. And if something like God was possible, it wouldn't be anything a human mind could come up with anyway."

Once she let go of trying to "know" so much, she could relax. "Now I just don't even think about it. It gives me peace being okay that this is all I know, and this is all I *can* know." There is integrity and ease for these Nones and Dones in finally speaking the truth about not believing religious dogmas.

No . . . Because Churches Hurt People

Some people disaffiliate or never join because they don't accept church doctrine. Others were pushed out. Lewis grew up in a large Black Baptist church in Atlanta. Looking back, the 38-year-old says his church ministered well with children, but they were completely out of step with teens.

"When *Harry Potter* was very popular, one of the preachers asked all the young people to the pulpit." To Lewis's horror, the minister demanded that they all make a public declaration that they would not read the *Harry Potter* series or engage in witch-craft. "Fourteen-year-old me was like, 'Are you bugging?' If you didn't read that, you didn't have anything to say during recess or lunch or anywhere else!"

More than the act of demonizing a cultural icon, Lewis felt the pastor was judging his whole generation. "You can't take all your kids and essentially shame them in front of their parents and the community. You're turning the church against them, and you turned us against the church. . . . Church has to be in a space to receive us, right? They have to create fertile soil that grows you and lets you change. They didn't know how to do that for us."

Jocelyn's evangelical church certainly made no room for her to grow or to be different. Now thirty-eight and living in New York, she was raised in a conservative, White, Christian home and extended community. "I was not a rebellious teenager," she said. "I was a leader in the youth group, homeschooled first through eighth grade in Colorado Springs." She attended Gordon College in Massachusetts, one of the premier evangelical schools in America. Every rule they laid out—including the dictates of purity culture, an evangelical movement emphasizing sexual abstinence before marriage, especially for girls—she followed to the letter.

During her college years, she realized the toll that obedience had taken on her body, mind, and spirit. "I'd been having panic attacks my whole life. And I chalked it up to, 'This is God speaking to you. It's God telling you you're doing something wrong, usually something about relationships and sexuality.' That's what the purity culture told me."

Once she traced the source of her pain, Jocelyn said she faced a moment of truth. "My choices were, 1) keep my worldview as it is and just be extremely unwell for whatever the duration of my life is, which probably won't be very long; or 2) turn everything upside down and rebuild. That was the catalyst for me to claw my way out of that evangelical fundamentalist mindset."

Like Jocelyn, Slater also had to escape Christianity for the sake of love and protection. Slater's mother is Tanana Athabascan from Alaska and was adopted as a child into a White family in South Dakota. Slater (who uses they/them pronouns) didn't know their father, except that he was Lakota. Slater's youth was entirely colored by their grandparents' White South Dakotan culture and community.

The family Lutheran church sat right behind their grandparents' house, though the family didn't attend very often. As Slater recalled: "Every once in a while, there'd be this resurgence, and we'd end up at church on a Sunday morning. It was very bizarre." A few times, Slater's mother took them to a nearby reservation for a powwow, but their White extended family discouraged any such engagement. "My grandparents were always speaking about Native people they saw in the news, and it was just a lot of racism."

From then on, at least for Slater, racism and Christianity were intertwined. It wasn't until Slater discovered more pathways into Indigenous spirituality and community that they felt free and whole. Now Slater is thirty-four, queer, lives in Minneapolis, and runs an organization that links young Indigenous people with their culture. It's the kind of community they never had and desperately needed as a child.

For so many of my conversation partners, the only path toward healing led away from church, especially when race and sexuality intersected with faith. Morgan is Black, twenty-seven, and was raised Baptist in Jamaica. As a teen, she attended a popular summer church camp and had a radical religious awakening. "There was this intense religious fervor," she said. "It was the first time I'd really internalized the idea of God loving me, and I was crying every day."

Unfortunately, the church group also taught her that God rejected homosexuality. "It sucked because the God they had given me could not love my friends. I didn't know how to work it out. Loving God does not mean I'm ready to give up loving my friends."

Her new Christian community insisted, so she chose her friends . . . and love. "That was it. Be Christian, believe in this God that said my friends are going to hell, or don't be Christian and just figure something else out. And so I spent the rest of my time in high school thinking, 'I guess I have no God.'" Today, she's a yoga teacher and student at Harvard Divinity School. She doesn't ascribe to a religion, though she said she trusts in the power of the world's religions to change society and change lives.

Craig is a 34-year-old White man and a drag queen in small-town Minnesota. He is a strong believer in changing society and minds, but he didn't start with that sense of empowerment and possibility. As a child, he was active in the family's Lutheran church in Fergus Falls, Minnesota. "We went because it was a community," he said. "It was all my relatives, a family stomping ground. Me and my close friend, who's actually also a drag queen now, we taught Sunday school together. I thought I might deliver sermons someday."

When he began to question his sexuality, he instinctively knew the church wouldn't welcome his ministry. "I heard those keywords of husband and wife, man and woman, traditional marriage. It was interesting to take that in and say, 'I don't fit in this picture. I don't fit in this thing they call religion.'"

Craig discarded Christianity but kept Jesus. "My spirituality came from looking at Jesus's practices: be kind to everyone, help those who need help, give that love, that compassion, that empathy," he said. "But my journey changed when I realized the church was about Scripture and getting it right, not about love."

Instead, Craig is finding creative ways to contribute to healing his community, including running a queer-friendly hair salon, organizing drag shows as Mrs. Moxie, and hosting a program on Northfield's radio station. There he talks about life, honesty, authenticity, and love. Those are the gifts he and many other Nones and Dones never received in the church, an institution they experienced as more adept at hurting than healing.

No . . . Because Church Isn't Worth the Trouble

Several of my conversation partners were disappointed because they actually wanted a deep spirituality and transformative action, and Christianity failed to deliver.

That was Alex's experience. She is White, thirty-one, married, lives in Atlanta, and remembers attending Catholic Mass regularly as a child, often on Saturday evenings. "It almost felt like, let's get it out of the way. Now we can sleep in tomorrow."

She enjoyed the family time, but she found it tough to take church seriously. "I don't remember a real emotional or spiritual connection. It just felt like a rite of passage. But I still remember praying before I went to sleep. I had this quiet conversation with God, who I envisioned as an older White man in the sky. Later, I just started to get really pissed off that I was sold such a narrow definition of religion, of God, of what spirituality could be."

Early on, Rhonda says she got the memo that she shouldn't expect much from church. She's twenty-one, Black-White, and attended a Lutheran church in Chicago as a child. It was underwhelming. "I would play on my Nintendo DS or be playing Pokémon," she recalled. "My parents, they didn't really care that much. And by the time I got to high school, I thought, 'It doesn't really matter.'"

Rhonda and Alex's religious upbringing syncs up with a pattern religion scholar Tara Isabella Burton notes in her book *Strange Rites: New Religions for a Godless World*:

> Today's Nones have grown up seeing religion as a social or communal institution—a "nice to have" teaching "good values" or solidifying family bonds—but not necessarily as a core part of their meaning or purpose. They're the kids who saw their parents attend church, or who went to Sunday school, but were nevertheless acutely conscious that their parents didn't actually believe all that stuff.[1]

Some young people followed in their parents' footsteps and stopped expecting more from church. Others felt cheated by the thin spiritual offerings and briefly tried to dig deeper on their own. Chris's family in Korea was moderately Catholic, and as a child, he hungered for more intense involvement. At age nine, he decided he would become an altar boy. He remembers it well: "I woke up at 5:30 a.m. every day for two hundred days by myself, learned the process."

Was it as spiritually nourishing as he hoped? "I didn't pay attention to sermons that much," he reflected. "It was kind of like a meditation for me."

Chris moved to Pennsylvania for school and was surprised at the American Catholic Church's judgment and exclusivity. "Here, they haven't evolved with the time," he said. "That's when I kind of realized, if God exists, it's one and the same God. I started to believe less in how you worship. It's more about your one-on-one relationship with God." Now he's thirty-one and living in San Francisco. His spiritual haven is the San Francisco Gay Men's Chorus, where he says they share creativity, commitment, community, and ritual.

David also found a more meaningful spiritual path after he left church. He's forty, Black, and teaches music at a high school in Minneapolis, but, for most of his life, he was an accomplished church musician.

"I was raised by my grandparents, and they were pastors at a small Pentecostal church in a small town in Wisconsin," he reflected. "Music was a gift God gave me, since I was little. So it would be me and Grandma. She was singing songs; I'd play the piano. That's how I connected with the divine or the holy or God."

At age eleven, he was playing at churches professionally. By the time he was sixteen, he had started his own music group and traveled the country. Then he hit the big time: worship pastor and music director for a Minnesota megachurch. He was at the top of the game, and he hated it. "I felt shackled in the church," he said. "I just got tired of playing for the same people, knowing they weren't hearing me. I wasn't growing. It was all a big show. I took a two-year hiatus once, and now I'm taking another break. I don't even know if it's a break. I don't know if I'll go back this time."

Instead, David shares God's love and connects with the public by playing music at the Minneapolis-St. Paul Airport. He said God feels more real to him there than in church (more on his spiritual practice in Chapter 4). "My connection with God now is way deeper," he said. "I'm no longer in a box. I'm no longer small-minded in my thinking and my approach. Anything that's good, anything that's making people's daily lived experience more positive, more bright, more beautiful—that's what I'm trying to do."

Latoya said she found plenty of spiritual nourishment in her childhood Black Southern Baptist church near Atlanta. Like so many young adults, she went away for college and the thread broke. These days, as a 41-year-old wife, mother, and attorney, she gets tired just thinking about trying to incorporate a faith commitment.

"Today? With two kids and my job?" she asked rhetorically. "I'd like my children to have that experience, but life is so busy, and Sunday is our one day of rest. My church growing up, I could be there from 11:00 a.m. to 3:30 p.m. I'm not looking for that experience today." She finds fulfillment in circles of women who share her love of running, yoga, being a mom, *and* praying for one another.

The church also showed up for Jax when he was young, and he is grateful for that connection. "I loved growing up there, and I still love all the people and the connections that I have," said Jax, who is Black-White, twenty-two, and lives north of New York City. "In some of the darkest points in my life, church people were the ones who came to visit me in the hospital."

He finally had to admit he found the whole church experience "just monotonous." "For so long I didn't understand it," he said. "My mom once tried to talk to me about what she got out of being a part of the church. I just realized, I found that through other things. So I don't really need it." Nones and Dones like Jax have no hard feelings against the church. They just can't imagine it being worth their time.

No . . . Because I Can't Be Labeled or Pinned Down

Several of my conversation partners solved the problem of religious ennui by adding more traditions and spiritual resources to their path and/or taking away restrictive labels. In many cases, they're not exactly nonreligious; they may in fact be uber-religious.

Take Martha, whose parents are from El Salvador and raised her in a strict Catholic household in Atlanta. "I've carried those traditions throughout my life as an adult as well, but they have progressed or evolved into something different and greater," she explained. "I think of myself as a syncretist" or someone who merges different religious and spiritual beliefs and traditions to form their own.

She's creative about honoring the different spiritual voices that inform her journey. "The challenge for me is being at peace," she said. "You can capture that peace through practices from different religions, especially Buddhism or Hinduism. It's about discovering what makes you feel whole, what's true for what you're feeling inside, and how to move forward. So yes, I also go to Catholic Church when my grandparents want to go. And my husband and I go to Grace [a nondenominational church]."

That combination might not make sense to others, but it is authentic for her. "I don't want to be labeled or limited. Based on my growing up, I saw a lot of judging from one type of Christianity to another. I don't want to be part of any of that."

Micah has also opted out of the church labeling game. His mother is an AME pastor, and he attends a theology school in Atlanta. But when I asked this 24-year-old Black man about his journey, he paused. "I'm Christian. That's probably about as far as I would go. I didn't really believe in God when I was in high school. Going into college, I went to church every now and then, because people invited me, but I didn't really have a reason to."

His path took a turn during the COVID pandemic, when he experienced a religious conversion. Even then, he maintained a fairly private relationship with God. "After my conversion, I was at 'Bedside Baptist,' watching church on my computer. Now I don't really have a church home, but I'm working for an Episcopal church, and I attend a Methodist seminary. I have no idea what religion I am."

He said he is comfortable with the lack of concrete religious identity. If anything, he feels well positioned to someday create spiritual, artistic expressions that reach beyond the church's walls.

Scholar Tara Isabella Burton refers to people like Micah and Martha as "religious hybrids."[2] They hold some of the beliefs and practices of one religion, but they feel content discarding the elements that don't serve their spiritual journey and/or adding spiritual elements, rituals, and even beliefs from other traditions.

Gael is thirty-seven, Latino, gender nonbinary, and takes pleasure in mixing, matching, and coloring outside spiritual lines. In other words, Gael is another of the hybrids. They are first-generation Mexican American and point with pride to their church, the majestic St. Mary's Cathedral in San Francisco. "I think the physical space, the beauty, the architecture, the aesthetic of that church had a huge impact on the rest of my life spiritually," they said.

Still, Gael wanted more. "Somewhere around the age of twelve, I started turning for answers toward—I'm not sure if the occult is the right term, but—toward myself and towards the earth. It was so nice to find a way to satisfy my own desires for a spiritual power that would come to my aid during difficult times."

All that may be true, but Gael also attends church periodically with their partner, who is a devout Christian. "Do I believe in God? Absolutely. What shape that takes, I have absolutely no idea and I'm okay with that," Gael said. "I have a lot of pagan-inclined grandmas and great-grandmas who were very Catholic, of course, but still carried Indigenous traditions and things like that. I like following in their footsteps."

Growing up, yoon never fit into the family Catholic Church. "I remember looking around and thinking, 'I feel like I'm missing something that everyone else has here. They seem so certain about what we're doing and purporting to believe, but I don't particularly feel anything.'"

For yoon, who is twenty-four, Korean, and gender nonbinary, the connections started to come when they discovered other religions. "I read about Hinduism, Buddhism, Judaism, Islam. I picked up little bit about pagan traditions and Western occultism, chaos magic, even existentialist philosophy." yoon loves being a student at Harvard Divinity School, in large part because the school is as pluralistic and label-defying as they are.

No . . . Because I Was Never Religious Anyway

Not every None is a Done who was raised in a faith and then departed. More and more often, Millennial and Gen Z Nones are growing up with no particular tradition. That doesn't mean they aren't seeking meaning, joining in spiritual practice, or forming meaningful communities.

Justin is twenty-four, Asian, and attends Santa Clara University, about an hour south of San Francisco. I met him while visiting scholar Elizabeth Drescher's class about nonreligious people in America. He laughed at the irony of essentially studying himself. "Yeah, my immediate family is not religious," he said. "I mean, I've always been around churches because of other family. Every time we have a family gathering, we're going to say grace. I've just never really explored it too much."

Justin sometimes meditates but has no regular disciplines. At this point in his life, he said, he isn't sure he needs them.

On the other end of the spectrum is Casper ter Kuile, a respected thought leader around contemporary, secular ritual (his book *The Power of Ritual: Turning Everyday Activities into Soulful Practices* was essential in my research). His passion is an admittedly personal one; he is thirty-eight, White, and a cradle None. As he told me:

> With most of the "Nones" conversation, there's a narrative of rejection and return. But I didn't start in a congregation, so it's never felt like a wounded home to me. It's just not my language. So going to a church building, for me, still feels like, "What are we doing here?" Especially when it's a smaller congregation, as is so often the case these days, the building is too big for the number of people, and there are all these gaps between them. If there's thirty of us, why aren't we in someone's big living room?

We'll hear more about Casper's spiritual practice—much of which involves large groups in his small Brooklyn apartment—in the very next chapter.

Like Casper, Caroline was raised in a religion-free household. She's twenty-five, White, and now lives in New York, but she understood early on that she was different from other children. "When I was in second grade, we had to do show-and-tell for the holidays, and we needed to say whether we were Christian or Jewish," she said. "So I asked my dad, 'Are we Christian or Jewish?' He said, 'You're a heathen.' That's what I told my class."

She continues to hold onto that identity, even as she acknowledges experiencing mystical awakenings. The most stirring happened while she was in college.

> I went to the Met exhibit in 2018, "Heavenly Bodies and Fashion in the Catholic Imagination." And I saw this dress and thought, "This is God. God is here." I had never thought to myself about what God might or might not be for me. I just saw this work of divine mystery and thought, "There's something in this fabric that is not a human creation. This is otherworldly." And I cried.

Sacred moments like that led Caroline to study religion and social justice in college. Upon graduation, she lived in an Episcopal young adult service community for a year. Church folk are eager to baptize her, but she doesn't know that it's necessary. Like so many Nones and Dones, she is comfortable with the mystery.

The Nones and Dones I met don't mind standing in a space of unknowing outside the confines of organized religion. It can be lonely. It can be confusing. It can also be energizing. Many have found it truly freeing to release ties to beliefs that seem unbelievable, to leave a community that has wounded you, to seek the spiritual depth your heart cries out for, to cast off labels, and to hold to whatever stance is truest to you. That doesn't mean God hasn't found a way to meet them where they are.

Seeking the Sacred

Question 2: How and where do you encounter the sacred?

Casper may be one of the most spiritual nonreligious people you'll meet. He was raised in England by Dutch parents who were avowedly secular. "Neither of my parents were religious," he said. "None of my grandparents were religious. So churchgoing was really not part of our cultural DNA, and God was not a subject of conversation. It wasn't anti-religious. It just wasn't any of that."

Still, he grew up embedded in ritual. He experienced it with his family: They attended a Dutch summer camp where the community would begin each day by gathering to raise the flag and sing together, followed by a "morning teaching." He experienced it at school: His parents sent him to a Waldorf school that incorporated the arts, academics, and nature, and strongly emphasized storytelling, community, and shared rituals. One place it didn't happen, and didn't need to happen, was in a personal faith community.

Casper's firm belief in the power of ritual and the need for social change led him to study at Harvard Divinity School. About ten years ago, he and classmate Angie Thurston made headlines when they published "How We Gather," a paper studying emerging generations and the secular spiritualities and communities they're creating. Today they run the Sacred Design Lab and help organizations and innovators to incorporate ritual and soulfulness into everyday life, culture, and community.

As someone who lives at the intersection of the religious and nonreligious, Casper reframes the idea of spiritual life in a way that Nones seem especially attuned to understand. He explained it beautifully in *The Power of Ritual*:

> We've been taught to see the world as divided between the sacred and the profane, the religious and the secular. We've been taught that there's somehow a line that makes a church building sacred and a supermarket secular. That vertical line is an invention. Instead, imagine a horizontal line between the shallow and the deep. It stretches across every place and every person. When we can sink below the blur of habit, we can be present to that portion of our experience where we find deepest meaning. Maybe it's poetry that takes us there. Or an incredible piece of theater. Or psychedelics. Or the arms of our beloved. Or simply watching our kids running through the yard. When we look at the world that way, any place and any time can be sacred. It all depends on how we look at it.[1]

Where are Nones and Dones like Casper discovering and drawing near to the sacred element present in all of life? What horizontal and vertical dimensions are they exploring, and how is the One many of us know as God meeting them beyond more explicitly religious spaces? My conversation partners touched on all those points as they responded to the second of my four queries: "How and where do you experience the sacred (sometimes alternatively phrased 'the holy,' 'the divine,' 'God,' 'mystery' and 'deep meaning')?" Before we hear those reflections, let's pause and establish a shared understanding of the word "sacred."

What Is Sacred?

As we've already noted, Americans overwhelmingly believe in God and a spiritual or sacred presence in the universe. But what do we mean when we say that, and how are we engaging with the divine? One of the benefits of asking dozens of people how they encounter the sacred or God is that many of them start by explaining what those terms mean for them. Their responses proved illuminating and at times provocative.

For Alex in Atlanta, the sacred is the deepest part of life. "The spiritual element," she said, "is almost like connecting with what is already here and understanding how we can honor life and live in a way that is in alignment with life." She makes that connection most profoundly when she engages in walking meditation and when she and her wife spend intentional, regular time with dear friends and neighbors.

Again and again, people spoke of the divine as a greater energy or power that is at once a part of us and something with which we can seek deeper connection. Stephanie—who is forty-one, White, and lives in San Francisco—said she understands the sacred this way: "I definitely believe that there is this God, this . . . I don't see it as a form, but there is this ultimate energy or source that we're all just pieces of. All humans, animals, plants—we're all made of the same stuff, and we all go back to that when we leave these bodies." She works as a hospice nurse or "death doula" (her title), and she is honored to be present as people return to that ultimate source when they die.

Arpan, thirty-three and Indian, lives in Atlanta and is quite matter-of-fact about spirituality, even if he identifies as agnostic. "We're human," he told me. "There's a physical level to us, there's a psychological level to us, and there's also a spiritual level to us. The goal is to find peace at all those levels." Meditation and journaling—especially about life's big questions—brings him to that place of peace.

Benjamin, a White 24-year-old California native who now resides in New York, has cultivated a diverse practice based on spiritual awakenings and global travel. One thing he has learned: "I think a lot of these [spiritual] forces are universal in some way. I don't feel like Jesus and the Buddha are on different teams at an absolute level."

Key has a similar approach to the sacred. She's twenty-three, Latina-Black, and lives in Minneapolis where she grew up in a Black church that felt like family. The welcome mat disappeared when she brought her girlfriend to church. Since then, she has developed a more expansive approach for talking to and about God.

"Believing in the universe is everything for me," Key said. "There's the galaxies, the moon, and the stars, and that sounds far away, but for me, it's almost as personal as somebody who is very religious and says, 'I walk with God every day.' For me, I definitely believe that the universe sits within me, that the universe is in every living thing."

Key's worldview in some ways reflects Taylor's Age of Authenticity or Smith's Millennial zeitgeist: She doesn't need to seek a higher source of authority grounded in a tradition, Scripture, institution, or even God; the universe is literally sitting within her.

As I listen to Key, I also hear a deep recognition that the universe is greater than her individual self and greater than any single one of us. She's trying to find a way to describe the immanence (it's in me) and transcendence (it's everything) of the holy. Those are worthy questions, and she told me she's hungry for spiritual teachers and mentors to help deepen her knowledge and practice.

If we're honest and generous, we can admit that there are countless ways to understand the sacred and holy. The Springtide Research Institute has been studying factors contributing to young people's emotional and spiritual flourishing for decades. They offer this definition of the sacred: "those things, places, or moments that feel special and set apart from others—experiences that evoke a sense of wonder, awe, gratitude, deep truth, and/or interconnectedness [to humanity, the universe or a higher power]."[2]

Their intentionally broad and secular definition might not please many theologians, but it is spacious enough to embrace the ways my conversation partners said they experience the holy. Based on their reflections, I've identified these common categories of spiritual practice:

- Connecting intimately with family, friends, and lovers
- Being creative and embodied, especially in music, dance, and art
- Engaging the natural world
- Reflecting in silence, especially through prayer, breathing, meditation, and journaling

- Meaning-making, as in reflection and reading
- Engaging expansive spiritual traditions
- Paying attention in a distracted world

Let's take a look at each type now, keeping in mind two things the Nones and Dones I met insisted on: Many of these practices might occur online or in-person, and any can be bundled with others and even combined with traditional church worship. As Martha explained in an unconscious summary of expressive individualism: "It's about discovering what makes you feel whole, what captures what you're feeling inside, and what helps you to move forward."

The Practice of Connecting Intimately with Others

Effie is twenty-one, Asian-White, and studies in Minnesota. Her face filled with sweetness when she spoke of encountering the sacred. "When I'm with my friends, I feel so thankful and connected, and that feels like a religious experience to me," she said. "I don't feel forced to say this is God in my friends. But that is how I encounter it now."

A 2023 Cigna study found that Gen Z is lonelier than any American generation: 58 percent of Americans feel lonely some of the time, but more than 70 percent of Gen Z sometimes feel lonely, and about as many feel no one knows them well.[3] It shouldn't be surprising that generations who suffer such high rates of loneliness would say they experience the sacred—feelings of wonder, awe, and gratitude, where they're both grounded and yet transcendent—when they finally connect with other people.

Still, the sheer volume of my conversation partners who named intimacy as a site for spiritual awareness gave me genuine pause. What's happening here? Are they experiencing more than the joy and comfort of being together? Are they truly naming something that is "of God"?

Victor broke it down for me during our visit in San Francisco:

> In Scripture, Jesus says, "Wherever two or more are gathered together, I'm there." Okay, there's more to it, because he says, "gathered together in my name," but I don't think that part is as important. To experience God, I don't think you have to be thinking explicitly about Jesus. This is *filia*, brotherly love. And that's a place where you're also sharing the experience of loving God.

Caroline in New York feels most connected to the divine when she's cooking, but even that moment is elevated when people she loves are involved. "Learning how to cook and eating a potato that your friend grew, that's spiritual," she said. "For me personally, cooking like that is my way of worshiping. It just feels better to eat a home-cooked meal when someone you love cooks for you. It feels better than if you ate that exact same food with the same ingredients, but someone who didn't care about you made it for you."

Victor and Caroline's experiences track with the Springtide report. In it, the researchers noted: "[R]elationships become the vehicle by which young people experience a sacred moment itself. Relationships help change moments from special to sacred."[4]

I appreciate this reminder that God shows up in our relationships. Whatever practice or activity you're engaged in, once you add more people—especially people with whom you share love, either for one another or for a shared cause—it can become sacred.

That's exactly how Flor, twenty-one, a White college student in Atlanta, described her encounters with the divine.

> When people are together and making music, there's something really strong in that. I feel something similar at protests, where there's the spirit of a bunch of people in one place doing one thing. It's really powerful. In fact, that's probably the most visceral connection I've had. I don't think I've ever had a moment of feeling the divine when I've been all alone. I don't think that happens for me. It's always when I'm with a group of people.

The difference may very well be that God, who is love, is made manifest wherever there is love between us. The first letter of John makes it clear: "Beloved, let us love one another, because love is from God, and whoever loves has been born of God and knows God. . . . No one has ever seen God; if we love one another, God abides in us and his love is perfected in us" (1 John 4:7, 12).

The Practice of Being Creative and Embodied

For Julia in New York, some of the most intense spiritual moments have come while she was singing or making art with other people. "When I was in church, and everyone started singing, I just felt so much warmth come over me," she recalled. "So whenever I experience live music or even just listening to music, I get that same feeling that church gave me."

She felt similarly moved back when she was a dancer. "I would always get lost in the moment," she said. "When you finally got the steps down and you're moving and breathing together, it's as if you're the same person or being."

The connection between the sacred and art is a rich and storied one. Dylan in New York is forty-two, White, a father of two, and a software engineer. During our interview, he showed me several of his sculptures and paintings. "This is how I connect spiritually now, through making art."

Like several of my conversation partners, he said psychedelic drugs further enhance that spiritual awareness. "If I'm using mushrooms while I'm making art, I can feel very connected to the world. I enjoy funneling my creativity that way. It's so clear I'm tapping into something bigger than myself."

Studying north of the city, Jax feels deep peace and connectedness when he is making or listening to music. "I find songs that have lyrics I really attach to, and those are my teachings," he said. "No, really—my bedroom is covered in song lyrics. I have a big cork board that's just printed-out song lyrics. I've made paintings of song lyrics."

What was it about those songs that made such an impact on him? "Often it's just songs reminding you that you're worth it. You're going to get through it. When you find that song, it feels like a wash of relief and profound joy."

The Practice of Engaging the Natural World

At least half of the Nones and Dones I met reported feeling closer to the sacred when they're in nature. Kelly left behind her Catholic faith a while ago, but when she's outside, the words of the faithful come rushing back, and she can't help but rejoice alongside all of creation.

"If I am in nature, I remember the Magnificat [Mary's song of thanksgiving to God]," she said. "My soul proclaims the glory of the Lord, and my spirit rejoices in God. It is a feeling of transcendence, belonging and not belonging in time and space, and recognizing the vastness of the universe."

You don't have to believe in God to share in these moments of profound gratitude and humility before nature. Erika, thirty-two and White, has been a leader in Atlanta's Sunday Assembly secular congregation for a few years. Her agnostic father shaped her outlook, and she's deeply grateful for that freedom.

"I once read a book that said, look at nature—there must be a God," she said. "And I thought, what's so beautiful to me is that it's so perfectly designed on its own as nature. Just the fact that there are the most beautiful places, the most unique animals, the way we've evolved. And, yes, it was a series of perfect little happenings, but those happenings *happened*. How perfect is that?"

For yoon in Cambridge, nature inspires a spiritual tug when nothing else can. "That's where I experience awe and reevaluate my place in the world and with the people around me." They described feeling that deep connection in 2024 during a total solar eclipse.

> It was beautiful, unlike anything I've ever seen, and it had an effect on me that I truly did not expect. I was speechless for half an hour after. I just kept thinking, "Wait, wait, wait." That may be one of the only instances of feeling I was outside my body or in the presence of something bigger than myself.

Nature offers us that sense of perspective and awe at the same time. When we behold the greatness and vitality of creation—and for some, the greatness of the God who made it—we're invited into right relationship with the rest of life. For once, it's not about domination or being human-centric. All things with breath and life are finally intertwined, one with another.

The Practice of Reflecting in Silence

Looking back on my own hilltop experiences in the natural world, each was also a moment for contemplation, awareness, attention to breath, and silent listening for a truth or a presence that rests beyond words. The Nones and Dones with whom I spoke craved this kind of silence. When they experience that stillness—through silent prayer, breath, or meditation—it is truly holy.

Lewis in Atlanta said prayer and silent conversation with God are essential to his spirituality, especially now that he no longer belongs to a religious community. "My spiritual practice is still rooted in praise and prayer," he said, "and none of those things necessarily have to happen in a traditional building."

"Daily prayer is important," he continued. "It's just me in my bedroom, praying when I feel I need to pray, acknowledging that my prayer is ineloquent but righteous. It's still heard. It's still received. It's not fancy words using the church formula, but I'm not trying to put God—or how I talk to God—in a box."

Grete understands spiritual practice as whatever "helps me engage in the world in a way that I can love people and take care of people and do good things and also love myself." All those commitments are easier when she is engaged in regular meditation at home in San Francisco. "When I sit and meditate a few days a week in the morning, if I'm just quiet with myself, I feel I can access something that's like a hum underneath everything."

Irina in Minnesota also appreciates how the energy shifts when she focuses on her breath. "I struggle with anxiety," the 21-year-old, White college student shared. "My therapist gave me this breathing exercise. You breathe in for four, hold for four, breathe out for seven. It's more for coping with anxiety, but I feel spiritual when I am mindful about my breath that way."

Many of my partners combine silent prayer or meditation with quiet journaling for a heightened experience of intimacy with the sacred. Arpan has been doing both for years.

> I meditate weekly—I have been for ten or fifteen years—and I find it very beneficial. I'm in my apartment, and I find a quiet place and make sure there's relatively low light. I'm just focusing on *pranayama* or breathing. A lot of times, I journal after I meditate, and it provides a lot of clarity. That's when I can ask the hard questions like, What is our purpose? Why are we here? And what actually makes you happy?

As my conversation partners have learned—and as Elijah discovered waiting for God on Mount Horeb (1 Kings 19)—silence often paves the way to a truth we couldn't have otherwise accessed.

The Practice of Making Meaning

Sitting with life's big questions and making meaning is itself a profoundly sacred practice. Rev. Katie Ernst, forty-one and White, serves as head chaplain at a private school in Minneapolis.

As an Episcopal priest, she's indisputably religious, but as a Millennial ministering with Gen Zers and their younger counterparts, Gen Alpha, she's deeply in touch with how young Nones and Dones encounter the holy:

> What's sacred for this community? I think this is true across every age group: questions of identity. Who am I? Who am I when there are competing forces either telling me or pushing me in a direction? Am I an athlete? An academic scholar? A theater person? An arts kid? Am I goth? Am I rebellious? Just a question of, who am I?

Sometimes they're exploring those questions on their own. Plenty of my partners turned to books, podcasts, and media from Eastern-influenced leaders like Thich Nhat Hanh and Sharon Salzbert, liberation theologians like Gustavo Gutierrez and James Cone, and assorted other spiritual biographies and self-help texts. A few told me they open the Bible when they have a heavy question or need to get re-grounded in their purpose.

Andy feels most spiritual and centered when he is doing things that rise from his core identity, including his work as a project manager for a San Francisco program for unhoused people. "I've always liked taking care of people, healing people," he said. "Working with the homeless population was the first time in my life that I really ever felt a sense of purpose, even when all I was doing was washing dishes. That connects me to spirituality."

Stephanie's vocation as a hospice nurse has also enriched her spiritual awareness. "Being with dying people, being in that liminal space with people, there's no way it can't be sacred," she said. "There's a spirit there, and you start to see that something is trying to liberate itself from this physical form."

Her calling rose from a profound confrontation with life's greatest unknown: death. "After my divorce, I had these panic attacks. I was so absolutely terrified and truly confronted with the fear of my mortality. Eventually I had to make peace with mortality and grief—they have so much to teach us."

As she discovered, transitions and changes of every kind inspire big questions and open doors for meaning-making.

The Practice of Expanding Spiritual Traditions

Slater awakened to the sacred only after stretching beyond White culture to embrace their Indigenous identity. Their world changed forever when a friend took them to the Sundance, one of Lakota culture's most sacred ceremonies.

"It's very strong, powerful energy," Slater said. "There's the thinnest veil between worlds, and during Sundance you're close to it. You bring that energy in and engage it in your body and then you put it back out into the world." Participating in that ancient ceremony was life-altering for them.

Unfortunately, living in the Twin Cities, Slater doesn't have easy access to Lakota community and ritual, so they create those opportunities within their two children at home.

> We have sage and cedar and sweetgrass, and we [burn the herbs and] smudge and offer prayer. It's a way to make the room feel like we're at Sundance or Inipi [the sweat lodge]. It's a grounding thing. I'll use the herbs on my heart to clear my head, clear

> my thoughts, and cleanse my heart and to help bring me back to myself.

Morgan lost access to her community's resources and rituals when she left behind church as a teenager in Jamaica. Later she discovered yoga and trained to become a yoga teacher. As she recalled:

> I learned how the physical practice of yoga is literally this tiny drop in the ocean. Everything else is the spiritual practice. That opened my mind and made me realize how cut off I'd been from the universe and from other people. It was my first time in over a decade of feeling that I understood something bigger than myself again, not just in an academic way, but in a way that touched my heart and that I could feel.

Like Morgan, many Nones and Dones—and plenty of people who consider themselves religious—tap into Eastern traditions for sacred wisdom and practice. They are also increasingly drawing on what might be called "New Age" beliefs and approaches. A 2017 Pew Research survey identified the top New Age beliefs as reincarnation, psychics, spiritual energy in physical things, and astrology.[5] According to that study, more than three out of four spiritual-but-not-religious people agreed with at least one of those beliefs. (Interestingly, six out of ten conventionally religious people agreed with at least one, as well.)

Pinning down a definition for New Age philosophy isn't easy. Some people tie it to Asian religion, because of references to reincarnation and meditation, but it's better understood as a late twentieth-century Western movement that pulls together beliefs in reincarnation, astrology, psychics, tarot, gemstones, magic, alternative medicine, and the presence of spiritual energies in the animal and natural world. The overall goal is to achieve human perfection and fulfillment and unity with all reality.

Those elements played out in several of my conversation partners' practices and perspectives. Gael in San Francisco has created their own unique amalgamation of practices, including incorporating Roman Catholicism.

> I find myself at my most powerful in the forest, in nature, and in magnificent spaces. I feel like my head is clear, and I can see the problem ahead. That is part of the gemstone work I do. It's also why I love going to Catholic Mass. Catholic churches tend to be more ornate, Baroque, Gothic, ancestral. I want all the gemstones. I want trees. I want to see humanity and the blood and sweat and history in the pews and how scratched they are and the gorgeous artistry all around. That is when I can really transcend and intuit my life more.

Rhonda in Minnesota feels strongly drawn to these New Age practices, as well. "I'm really into manifestation," she said. "That means believing in my desired reality, having the mindset of who I want to be and trusting that will lead to having the life I want."

She looked a little sheepish, but I encouraged her to go on. "I know it sounds nonsensical, if I think about it logically," she said. "But I found some YouTubers that I really like talking about it. And I got into tarot card reading at one point. I love astrology. So it's kind of all over the place."

Rev. Ryan Kuratko is forty-two, White, and serves as the Episcopal chaplain at Columbia University. He said church folk would probably be surprised at how often students like Rhonda come to him.

"Over the last couple of years, more than anything else, it's been tarot," he said. "Everybody's getting tarot card readings. I actually have a spiel now about it." He went on to share:

> My standard answer is that tarot offers a rich symbolic language for negotiating the spiritual in your life. To the extent you think you're controlling something, it's not that helpful. But the extent to which the cards and the rich symbols make you reflect on where you've experienced difficulties in real life or how you are in relationship, that's helpful.

As we saw in Chapter 2, Millennials and Gen Zers have access to a spiritual marketplace more robust and accessible than previous generations could imagine. The Nones and Dones I met don't hesitate to draw on that diverse storehouse as they seek the sacred.

The Practice of Paying Attention in a Distracted World

My conversation partners also shared about the importance of crafting a healthy relationship with the internet and digital social media. Effectively managing screen life is a spiritual practice in itself. And an unhealthy relationship with your iPhone can cancel out the benefit of nearly every other spiritual practice.

Liam in New York could feel social media's negative influence on his peace of mind and knew it was time to change. "I ended up nuking my Twitter account," he said. "I realized, oh crap, my mental health is in the tubes because of this. Later I did it with Instagram. Everything tech-wise is trying to guide you into this sort of compulsive consumption that you can't control."

California college student Justin hasn't taken that drastic a step yet, since he's not drawn to social media (though the games on his phone occupy a lot of his time). He wonders about the power of the computer in our pockets to draw us away from real life. "I was reading something for a class just last night, about the idea of boredom," he said. "People just immediately go on their phone if they're bored or they feel this fear of missing out on things. They can't let it go."

He was especially alarmed when he sat near a young woman on a flight and watched her spend two hours editing her own portrait photo. "I thought, okay, this is not healthy."

My Gen Z conversation partners in particular were eager to share their strategies for reducing screen time. They regularly track the number of hours a day they've spent on their phones. New York college student Basil—a White 20-year-old who hails from Arkansas and uses they/them pronouns—sets time limits within their apps, so they can't spend half the day mindlessly scrolling. "There's just other things I would rather be doing that are a lot better for my eyes and for my brain and for my heart," Basil said. "I don't need to be attached at the hip with this thing."

Alex in Atlanta called my attention to Jenny Odell's *How to Do Nothing*.[6] The book inspires readers to resist the "attention economy," or the way businesses and digital platforms vie for our attention in order to increase engagement, revenue, and influence. "Our culture has fostered such fragmented attention," Alex told me. "It's bad for democracy because we can't build and sustain anything together. We can't stick with something and persist when things get tough. This book is about us reclaiming our agency by slowing down and attending to less of that noise."

Quieting the urgent siren song of digital and media culture has helped many of the people I met connect with the sacred. That's why Dylan turned off Facebook back in 2016. "It was right after Trump won the first time," he said. "I just thought, 'I can't be fed a steady diet of this.'"

More than politics, he was troubled by the feeling that his attention was always split. "I've realized there's a very important aspect of purity of experience that can't be filled with competing messages and competing things. That's now something I strive for in my life—some sense of purity and being in one place at one time." He and his wife are in New York raising two boys, ages eight and ten. "That's something I want to reinforce with them. Paying attention to what's right here."

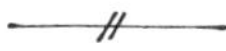

The young Nones and Dones I met definitely aren't religious in the traditional sense. Very few experience church worship as sacred. They might speak of God, Jesus, the universe, or use no names at all. But make no mistake: Hunger for the sacred is very much alive in their midst. It's just filtering through the lens of the Millennial zeitgeist, which prioritizes nonjudgment, inclusion, individuality, pluralism, fluidity and freedom.

That's certainly true for Atlanta lawyer and mom Latoya. "As you live in the world, you see it's so much bigger, and there are so many ways to feel connected spiritually," she said. "It's beautiful because everyone doesn't have to be a sit-in-a-pew, receive-a-message person. That may not be the way for everybody, but it doesn't mean their spirituality is less worthy."

Whether they're singing or silent, reading or praying, exploring nature or making meaning, alone or together, these Millennials and Gen Zers have taken spirituality out of the box. They feel free to seek mystery, awe, wonder, gratitude, and meaning in every moment and every place. Church folks might discover a fresh blessing if we sought the Spirit's movement with such freedom and abandon.

Building Community While Bowling Alone

"Nothing left but each other." The words are inscribed on a sticker on Flor's laptop. They're also on a dog tag hanging from her neck. "It's one of my real guiding phrases," the 19-year-old explained. "There may not be a lot that we can do, but what we can do is with each other." She has come to this knowledge the hard way.

Flor hails from the Midwest, where her mom serves as an Episcopal priest. She attended church regularly as a child and still holds that community dear, but she was also grateful to get some space when she headed to college in Atlanta a couple of years ago. Sadly, the isolation she experienced in high school also surfaced when she arrived at college.

"I'm doing everything I can to fight that loneliness because last year and the year before that and all throughout high school, I did feel so lonely," she said. Oddly enough, she felt less alone when the pandemic struck and her school went virtual. "It should have been super lonely and isolating, but I started up a Minecraft server with a bunch of friends, and we had that connection and friendship all the time. A lot of my activism and organizing now stems from that experience of being in a group that came together and cared about each other."

That memory eventually lit a fire and inspired her to connect with people at college, and her efforts are finally bearing fruit.

> It feels good to remember I actually do have the power to get people together and figure out what we can do to make things better. There's a few of us that are working together on a communal dinner. We're also really interested in mutual aid networks—it's a framework of building communities that help each other, not just friends or people you get along with, but different people bring skills or just a voice that's needed in the community, and they share.

Even if those big dreams don't pan out, Flor can already feel the difference community makes in her life. "That's one of the places I find divinity—it's in each other and in the things that we can do for each other," she said. "I'm the happiest I've been in a long time because I'm starting to have good networks and connections like this."

—//—

Millennial and Gen Z Nones and Dones regularly battle with loneliness and isolation, so they have a keen sense of the human need for social networks. That's why it felt so important to pose my third query: "How and where do you experience community and belonging?" Many of them are creating and leaning into alternative sources of community, but just as many have stalled out, unsure how to connect and belong beyond their intimate circles.

We will hear both perspectives in this chapter, starting with the struggle for authentic community in a culture of isolation and privatization. Then we will turn to their stories of fending off loneliness and gathering in meaningful community.

How Do You Build Community When Everyone's Bowling Alone?

Only a few sessions into my interviews with young adult Nones and Dones, I noticed a disturbing pattern: People didn't have much trouble with private spiritual practice, but not nearly as many were discovering a deep sense of belonging and community. After the fourth interview, I sat in the car, hung my head, and fought to control a wave of sadness. Their struggle was palpable, and my heart broke for them.

Stephanie in San Francisco was one of the first and most honest to share about her hunger. "Something I've been yearning for is community, that sangha or that group of people who participate together in the teachings and in service together," she said. "I can get pretty excited about reading philosophy and spirituality on my own, but integrating it and practicing it? To have that, you need the people. Give me some people!"

The hospice nurse regularly practices at a yoga studio and said she has made a few "sweet" connections with classmates.

> But deep meaningful community, I would say I don't have. I have two really solid friends in the Bay Area that I feel I can call upon. I have my partner. But I don't feel there's a place

> where I could say, "This is home, and these are my people." The older I get, and another year has passed where I'm not a part of something, I wonder, do I even still know how to go about this?

Several people named the difficulty of finding a community when you don't have children, are no longer a student, and don't have a faith tradition. There's no guarantee you'll feel true belonging in a parents' group, at school, or at church, but it's even harder when you don't have access to any of those ready-made circles.

Community can be an even greater challenge for Millennials and Gen Zers, because your twenties and thirties are marked by transience and transition. Julia had a steady group of friends in college. Now twenty-five and living in New York, she can't find a place or a way to belong.

> I would love to be in a community, but for now it's something I'm grasping at. I had it with friends at school. When I was younger, it was also cool to see at church—this group of people who wouldn't necessarily know each other, who are basically strangers, but they support each other in a time of need and come together as a community. I don't have that at this present moment.

Nemo is forty-two and moved to San Francisco from Serbia about seven years ago. He is a fixture in Yoga on the Labyrinth at Grace Cathedral and is also a member of a meditation and qigong (martial arts) group, but he isn't sure those are his communities. "It's one thing to have a group of people," he said. "It's something more to have community. Casual is easy. It's not a substitute for real substance."

He is also struck by the cultural differences between Eastern Europe and the United States. "I can honestly say this is not an easy society to get more deeply connected. You have so much freedom of expression, but it's not easy to approach someone's private life."

Jocelyn in New York is a self-proclaimed introvert and doesn't apologize for guarding her "me-time." She also conceded she may be too comfortable being alone. "It is harder for me to make myself go out and do stuff," she said. "And I don't know how much of that is, I got so used to not doing it during [pandemic] lockdown and now that's just how I am. Or do I prefer being alone, because it is genuinely harder for me to be social? I'm not sure."

Breaking out of our isolation chambers is even harder when you consider the impact of cars, television, internet, and cell phones, all of which contribute to the narrowing of our physical worlds and walls. Add the attention economy we referenced at the end of Chapter 4—where entertainers and businesses all conspire to keep our eyeballs and ears glued to their content day and night—and it's no wonder we can't put down the devices long enough to connect with God or one another.

Pluralization and the era of infinite possibility both complicate the process of finding and forming community. On the one hand, as yoon in Cambridge pointed out, they can now track down fellow Korean gay men around the world and share stories, wisdom, and laughter online. But yoon said that doesn't nurture their soul the way IRL ("in real life") relationships do. "It tends to be a lot more individualistic than I would like," they said. "I wish it were more communal."

In addition, as Martha in Atlanta discovered, pluralization enables her to assemble spiritual practices from a wide range of global sources. What's the downside? She said, "It's difficult to find people who are open to weaving different things, too." Once you've crafted your own specialized spiritual path, no one tells you how to find the people who also share your unique set of passions. You can bounce from one interest circle to the next without feeling truly at home anywhere.

Grete in San Francisco believes communities of solidarity and mutual support will be more vital in the near future, given today's changing political winds and the vulnerability of people of color, women, LGBTQIA+ people, and poor people.

> Going into this year [2025] with the new federal administration, I'm just feeling clear that we are the ones who save us. I think salvation, not in an afterlife way, but in this lifetime on this earth, comes through each other and taking care of each other. I want to find and build a community that is interdependent like that.

Had she ever experienced such a community? She sighed. "Church was that for me, but it was conditional. As long as I was within their norms, they would take care of me. But as soon as I stepped out of those norms or had different beliefs, it was over." I heard the same deep sense of grief and loss in the stories of so many conversation partners. They have no desire to return to Christianity, but they miss their church family.

Others described a different struggle: they feel skittish about being boxed in or limited by a particular community or identity. So while they yearn for spiritual depth and an abiding sense of belovedness and belonging, when the opportunities arise, they feel they can't make time and don't want the labels that come with institutions.

Millennials and Gen Zers aren't the only ones averse to this kind of commitment—the forces of privatization and pluralization have given us all less community than we need and more choices than we can manage. But at least among the younger subset I met, there's heightened wariness around being coerced and manipulated by religious communities and their leaders.

Younger Americans also feel less cultural pressure to join or commit to much of anything. They are waiting longer to marry and have children, if at all. They're moving more regularly to new jobs and even new career paths (partly because companies stopped making long-term commitments to workers and instead encouraged the shift to an often exploitative gig economy). Lots of Gen Zers and Millennials want community. It's genuinely countercultural to overcome institutional distrust and habit enough to commit to one.

These realities made me even more curious about people like Flor who are scaling the walls of loneliness and creating the nonreligious communities they and others desperately need. Where and how are they developing that sense of community and belonging? For the people I met, it could happen in-person or online, and most likely in these contexts:

- Belonging with chosen family
- Belonging around music and the arts
- Belonging in fitness and yoga groups
- Belonging at work
- Belonging in an alternative worship community

Let's hear about these possibilities and realities from the Nones and Dones themselves.

Belonging with Chosen Family

When Lewis in Atlanta needs to feel grounded and beloved, he heads to the Village. It's not a place; it's a close friend group who've known each other since they were kids. "We were all similarly raised, either Baptist or CME [one of the historic Black denominations] or AME or Holiness-Pentecostal," he said. "We could play at church if we wanted to. Now we know better than to do that. So we call ourselves The Village, and we keep each other rooted in a lot of ways the church would have done for us."

When someone has a health scare, the Village prays. When somebody wants to play cards or board games, the Village sets the table. When someone suffers a breakup, the Village gathers 'round, often virtually but still powerfully. "We support each other, pray for each other. As the elders would say, we shepherd each other."

Alex is also in Atlanta and is blessed to have something like a Village of her own. Circles like this don't just materialize without effort. "My wife Kyla is so good at maintaining relationships over time in a way that I am not," she admitted. On the day we sat to talk, Alex was preparing to see friends who participated in her wedding a few years ago. There's now a circle of ten adults and a growing group of kids, and they all tend to one another. "We're going to visit tonight, and we're bringing them soup. It's amazing, the repetitive act of showing up for each other in small ways. This is what it's all about, you know?"

Those circles—some call them "chosen family"—can include people you've grown to know and love over time. Caroline in New York took a risk and placed herself in a position where she had to sink or swim with strangers in a young adult service program. In the end, she didn't just find a community. She found God.

> I lived in intentional community for a year. Honestly, it made me realize God is in people. At the beginning of the year, we had to write intentions and hang them on this tree. And I wrote, "I want to know God." Throughout the year, I got to know the people around me so excruciatingly well, whether or not I liked them. And I thought, "They are God, God is in them." I realized God is in the difficulties and the nuances of engaging and interacting with another person. I'm so grateful knowing that's what community can be for me.

Belonging around Music and the Arts

Lots of my conversation partners feel deeply rooted in communities centered on music and art. For Chris, the San Francisco Gay Men's Chorus *is* church. "That's my community. We take care of each other like family, so even if I don't know somebody, there's an affection because we're both in this community." The chorus is a serious commitment: Members attend two rehearsals a week, and some have been in the circle for decades. He also loves that the group encourages activism and inspires local and national social change.

Perhaps because of its life-affirming presence during the AIDS crisis, the chorus has developed a host of rituals to celebrate transitions, honor elders, and bless one another. Chris finds these intentional moments especially meaningful.

> Every time before a concert, we are given a piece of paper that has names of the "fifth section"—the members who are now dead. So we hold hands and sing an Irish blessing for them and then we go out. It gives me chills. We all believe in it. It's almost like we have a religion. There's a force that drives and holds us together.

Music held Jax together when he suffered a severe depression not long ago. More than just listening, he found solace, strength and belonging among fellow concert-goers who gathered to share in a powerful collective experience.

> Most of the artists I listen to, a lot of the audience struggles with the same things that I did. So at the concerts people go around giving away these themed friendship bracelets. Or we're making a bunch of pieces of colored paper to put in front of your phone flashlight on a specific song. The community puts so much effort and care into that shared experience.

Jax went on to tell me about a moment of deep vulnerability and connection during a recent Twenty One Pilots concert.

> I was alone but I didn't feel alone. It was great being around people who all felt the joy of seeing them. And there's a song off their first album, where the chorus asks the friend to remove your hands from over your eyes. It says something like, I know

you want to leave, but friend, please don't take your life from me. When you're standing in a crowd of people who've either been that friend or the friend who is asking, "please" . . . Wow.

What is it about music—especially music in the context of community—that elevates us and facilitates such an overwhelming sense of healing and belonging? French sociologist Emile Durkheim would say we're experiencing collective effervescence.[1] That's when a group of people gather for some activity—anything from a religious ritual to a concert, a drag show to a street protest—and together enter into a shared emotional, energetic state and forge a common identity.

Music is an especially effective conductor of collective effervescence because it taps into our emotions and provides a rhythm everyone is literally humming to or moving with. If the musician also offers meaningful lyrics or a narrative people can connect to their own lives, you might soon have more than fans. You could have a dedicated, even transformative community (shout-out to Taylor's Swifties and Beyonce's Beyhive).

David said he tries to create those moments on an intimate level when he plays music at Minneapolis-St. Paul Airport.

> Most people at the airport are going through something—heading to a big family event, coming home from deployment. And as I sit there and play, I can feel the heaviness of everything we're all going through. But I also feel I'm supposed to be in that space with them, to create something that makes us all feel more free, alive, vibrant. I have community that way.

As he considered that experience of togetherness, he went a step further: "Really, for me, community is every time I see a whole Black audience doing the Electric Slide, dancing and being free. Every time I see students coming together, creating their own music, singing songs, lifting their hearts, lifting the room. It's just all those times."

Craig feels the same freedom and connection when he—or should we say his alter ego, Mrs. Moxie—hosts drag shows in Northfield, Minnesota. The diverse community they've nurtured is unlike anything he's ever known.

> I've had people of all kinds come to shows and say, "This is the first time I felt joy." I don't want to say drag is like church, but maybe it is. It brings people to a building together in a safe place. It entertains people. It helps them forget their worries. The last thing I want you to think about when you're at my show is that you have radiation on Monday or you have the mortgage on Friday. I want you to leave all your worries and be present and authentic, and just enjoy and laugh, which is what heals the soul the most.

In their paper "How We Gather," Casper ter Kuile and Angie Thurston describe several arts-based secular communities where Millennials feel deeply connected. Casper and his husband have seen it for themselves: They host a monthly community singalong in their Brooklyn home.

"We have a one-bedroom apartment, but we've fit seventy people in it," he laughed. "Singing together with people is really important to my spiritual life. My favorite thing is watching people who come for the first time just saying, 'What is this?' They really appreciate it."

Music, art, dance, movement—when people gather to share these practices, community and belonging will often follow.

Belonging in Fitness and Yoga Groups

When I asked friends and colleagues where they think nonreligious people find community, most listed fitness and yoga. Picture a high-end, high-commitment fitness studio where the class leader barks commands and affirmations in equal measure. The walls are covered with posters like this one for Equinox gyms: "Commit to Something." Or maybe it's this Peloton slogan: "Motivation That Moves You." Thankfully there's a low-rent option from Blink Fitness: "Every Body Happy." And wherever you pursue those goals, Nike wants to make sure you "Just Do It: Dream Crazier."

These businesses are tapping into something humans have understood for centuries: the synergy between spirituality and embodied fitness. People today may simply be transferring their desire for ritual, self-improvement, discipline, and community from the church to the gym.

Darren Main is honored to serve what may be the best of both worlds. For more than fifteen years, he has taught Yoga on the Labyrinth at San Francisco's Grace Cathedral, which gathers hundreds of people every Tuesday evening and Saturday morning. Though Darren is a few years beyond the Millennial threshold (he's fifty-three), he leads a practice community filled with younger Nones and Dones and finds himself serving as their counselor, spiritual director, and teacher.

He didn't start out hoping to shape a community of meaning and belonging, but for many of his students, that's what happened.

> A lot of people would just come to do exercise, or because the music is great and the architecture is fantastic. Then they started to have these very emotional experiences, and I would hear them slowly talk about how this is a counterpoint to whatever abuse or struggles they had experienced in church. You just feel open, in touch with a part of yourself that is bigger and more beautiful than you thought possible. And what human doesn't want that?

Darren doesn't press hard for the community connection, but I experienced gentle nudges when I joined the yoga circle at Grace at the outset of my travels. He created a welcoming atmosphere for everyone, making sure we knew all bodies and abilities were welcome. He spoke about a theme he'd been pondering—that day, it was "attention"—and how we might reflect on it during class and afterward in our daily lives. He invited the Cathedral's dean, The Very Reverend Malcolm Young, to offer a word of welcome and to take off his collar and join in. Near the close of class, Darren encouraged us to turn and introduce ourselves to the people around us.

He is aware that the Grace yoga group is the primary spiritual community for a lot of participants in that circle.

> Some people can go solo and live in a cave—good for them. The rest of us need something that holds you while you explore and grow. Most of us need community. We need a safe space

> where we're seen and felt and known. I strive to create that. Whether or not you touch your toes is irrelevant to me. You feeling safe enough to touch something within yourself—that's what matters.

One of Darren's former students, Benjamin, has taken part in spiritual communities around the world. Today he lives in New York, but his deepest experience of community to this day is with a multi-generational meditation group he met through Darren just before the pandemic.

> So it was me and four other people: one is in his sixties, one in her thirties, two in their forties, and me [about twenty at the time]. The five of us would sit, meditate, and teach on Zoom every week for the whole pandemic. It was one of the most alive transmissions that's ever come through me. When we reconnect, I don't even like all of them, to be honest. There's this personal level where I know, "I'd never hang out with you, but I love the shit out of you, and I could just sit with you for hours." Even though we're all in such different worlds, there's a feeling of community.

At the other end of the spectrum, Latoya in Atlanta shares plenty in common with her fitness community. Those initial affinities have opened the door to a truly sustaining sisterhood.

> I have such a community with my women's run group. We're running but there's also yoga and mindfulness. We focus on making time for our self-care and health and encouraging one another and sharing wisdom with one another. We create

> opportunities for each of us to go further—if you've run a 5K, think about joining a group of us who are getting ready for our first half marathon.

Latoya started the group with a couple of friends, and now it has blossomed to include nearly fifty women. Some of them are also part of her moms' circle. "We have our group chat, and we're constantly supporting each other as moms with articles, tips, or resources. I pray for them, and I know they pray for me, whether it's in the chat or on a call."

She is well aware that her spiritual community doesn't look like anything she imagined growing up in the Black Baptist Church. "I'm just finding community where I can," she said, "still loving the Lord and living my life as someone who's very spiritual and a believer, but not in the traditional way." For Latoya and plenty of others, moving our bodies with intention moves us closer to one another and to the sacred.

Belonging at Work

Considering the amount of time most of us spend at work, it's good to know deeper community can form in that context. Craig spends his spare time organizing drag shows in Minnesota, but his day job running Queenie's salon also provides ample opportunity to build relationships and community. "I absolutely find community and belonging within my business as a hairdresser," he said. "People think of us as therapists because we are there to listen."

Andy's life changed when he started working for a program serving unhoused people in San Francisco. "Sometimes it's wild to think where I was and where I am now," he reflected. "If you would have asked when I was homeless, I was starting to think that was going to be it for the rest of my life."

Having work with a purpose and people who share it—for Andy, those were the gamechangers. "I'm pretty happy," he said. "I love what I do. I love the people I work with, the community we serve. Belonging is something that a lot of people lack, and it's a hard thing to put your finger on. All I know is, I really feel I belong where I'm at right now."

When I spoke with Dylan in New York, he had trouble talking about community and belonging. Then the light bulb clicked on: "I feel it in my job." He works for an IT firm that specializes in supporting progressive movements. "I've been there for about two years now. That has become a community of people that I really love and trust and respect."

Most of the staff are remote, but he said they've taken great care to build more than a workplace where you clock in and out online.

> We do quarterly meetups, go on retreats, and see each other in real life, all of which is important. Honestly, it's unlike any tech company I've ever seen: diverse genders, races, identities. I draw a lot of strength from it, and I'm protective of them. We all help each other. And it matters that I'm part of the group shaping the culture and defining what the company is. I do feel a strong sense of belonging and purpose, because I'm helping to create it.

Work can be a literal chore, or it can be a primary location for belonging. These Nones and Dones are choosing to infuse their work with meaning and community.

Belonging in Alternative Worship Communities

Several of my nonreligious conversation partners are cultivating relationships in an unexpected place: a worship community. Just because you're a None or Done, that doesn't mean you don't attend worship periodically. Remember that, according to the Pew Center's research, some 10 percent of religiously unaffiliated people report attending anywhere from once a week to a few times a year.[2]

Kimberley, the interfaith chaplain in Philadelphia, said she still feels very much at home when she visits her mother's small church in Maryland. She doesn't need to agree with them to feel connected. That said, she also values a spiritual community she discovered during pandemic: the digital hush harbor, named after the outdoor "hush harbors" where enslaved people secretly gathered to worship and preach apart from the slave master's theology and influence. As Kimberley explained it to me:

> A lot of other Black women have been on the journey of decolonization, where we were raised Christian, but started having more questions and feeling more distance in the rise of evangelicalism connected to Trump and things like that. So these digital hush harbors, as we call them, they meet with some regularity on YouTube or other private platforms.

They might feature a worship-like experience, including prayer and a leader who offers a message, but there's also lots of engagement in the chat. Everyone's voice matters in the digital hush harbor. Some communities also host more intimate, follow-up Zooms for deeper discussion and relationship-building. Liberating virtual gatherings like this have been a godsend for Kimberley.

Arpan also went online to find a doorway to meaningful community. Growing up in Birmingham, Alabama, his family were regulars at the Hindu temple, but he drifted away once he got to college. "As I got older, I started to realize I was lacking a sense of community, and I really wanted to have that," he said. "So I did some research and found out about Sunday Assembly Atlanta through Meetup.com."

What is Sunday Assembly? Founded in 2013 by two English comedians who craved a secular, inclusive church experience, it's now a collective of about forty secular communities across the United States and the United Kingdom. The Sunday Assembly Atlanta website announces: "We are a secular community that celebrates this one life we know we have. Our motto is to 'live better, help often, and wonder more.' We wish to help everyone reach their full potential."[3]

Sunday Assembly has no doctrine or dogma, but when I attended one of the Atlanta group's monthly gatherings, it looked and felt a lot like traditional worship . . . with some important differences:

- Greeters are waiting to warmly welcome you and get you settled with a nametag. You can also grab a Sharpie and a card and write down either something you're celebrating or something that's got you concerned.
- They start with a potluck meal at small tables. If you don't know anyone, don't worry—someone will invite you to a table.

- Eventually, band members leave their tables to gather up front and play a set of pop songs like "Hold My Hand" by Hootie and the Blowfish and "Imagine" by John Lennon—inspiring and meaningful songs that would get you thinking or smiling if you heard them on the radio. The theory: If you'd sing it in the car, why not sing it with this group?
- After a few songs, a leader takes the mic to read the cards with everyone's concerns and celebrations. The whole group snaps fingers, nods, or even claps depending on what's been shared.
- They also announce a variety of community activities: volunteer opportunities, a small group to talk philosophy, picnics in the park, and much more.
- Then it's more music, more community, and general friendliness (and excellent homemade ice cream).

Arpan only joined the Assembly recently. When he noticed there was no intentional space for discussing spirituality and philosophy, he offered to start a small group. "I've always enjoyed reading philosophy and having those deep conversations," he said, "and it was easy to start a small group within the larger group. I can do a lot on my own, but that kind of community—that was the one missing piece for me."

Erika has been a Sunday Assembly regular for about three years. She now organizes the community's volunteer efforts across Atlanta, an important way to connect with their neighbors and also to dispel the misconception that humanists and atheists don't serve others. As Erika shared:

> People are sometimes still surprised when we show up. Sunday Assembly is where I am getting that chance for personal

> growth and reflection, but also where I'm driven out into community. I mean, I love my Dungeons and Dragons group. That's a great, fun, tight-knit small world. Sunday Assembly is out in the world, trying to make connections.

She never expected to commit so deeply to this or any group. "I'm not a joiner, but . . . well, that's the thing with us. Sunday Assembly is trying to be a community for people outside of church."

Lots of Westerners who leave church turn toward Eastern religions and philosophy. When Liam shifted from The Episcopal Church to study Buddhism, he didn't stop with reading and meditating alone. He said he was eager to join a sangha, or practicing community.

> The sangha is an integral part of Buddhist practice. When we do the Vandana and Tisarana every week—they're both a chant and a statement—we are basically saying, "I go to the Buddha for guidance. I go to the dharma [or teaching] for guidance. I go to the sangha for guidance." In the United States, people bring this individualistic frame to Buddhism, but it's always about community.

That's a message Rev. Katie Ernst shares regularly at the Breck School in Minnesota. As the senior chaplain, she leads an interfaith community that includes students from preschool to high school, plus a diverse faculty and staff. She's an Episcopal priest, but she can't assume everyone is Christian.

So the first gathering of every year, she offers what she calls a litany of belonging. "We welcome everyone," she said. "I call out as many groups as I can conjure up. I try to imagine everyone who's there and what they need to hear, to know they're being seen." That includes an intentional welcome to people of every faith and no faith.

Ernst crafts the statement at the start of the year; after that, students take turns leading the litany of belonging. "They're standing up here and I'll ask, 'Who's the person that makes you feel okay and loved?' Sometimes they'll name a deity, sometimes they'll name a mom or grandpa. And I'll say, 'Imagine they're standing next to you, and you're projecting that welcome to this whole group.'"

Many of the young people and adults in her care may not have any other opportunity to access community, meaning, and belonging. She's determined to keep that door open as wide as possible.

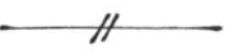

Humans will keep evolving, but we won't outgrow our need for community. That's why so many Millennial and Gen Z Nones and Dones are determined to form it: at work, in the neighborhood, in shared creative spaces, in alternative worship gatherings, in fitness groups, and in other spaces we haven't touched on.

Even among those who aren't rooted in a community, most still want one. Whether they've left behind faith, or they never had it at all, whether they're scared to commit or ready to go all in, these Nones and Dones expressed genuine yearning for a community that shares meaning, cultivates belonging, serves others, and, yes, deepens their awareness of the sacred. What they need now is help creating and sustaining it in a culture that discourages connection and commitment.

PROPHESY TO THE BONES

I will pour out my spirit on all flesh;
your sons and your daughters shall prophesy,
your old men shall dream dreams,
and your young men shall see visions.
Even on the male and female slaves,
in those days I will pour out my spirit.

—Joel 2:28–29

When God wants to wake people and speak a word of truth, the odds are good that God will work through people on the edge. The young and very old. Slaves and women. Poor people and outsiders to power. Ezekiel received his first vision at age thirty. Jesus was about the same age when he burst from the wilderness to turn the synagogue and the world upside down.

My hunch when I hit the road was that God might be speaking a word to our churches through emerging generations of Nones and Dones. I framed the fourth and final question—"What would you tell the church or organized religion, if we were listening?"—in order to directly solicit their insights. In the four brief chapters that follow, you'll hear that wisdom for yourself.

The speakers wouldn't have called their messages a prophecy, but I believe we can receive them as such. Like the prophets of old, my conversation partners sometimes *called the church out* of its self-protective, self-preserving, and selfish behaviors. They also *called the church in* to more holy, generous, vibrant, and relational ways of being. These prophecies—whether they're phrased as a fierce calling out or a generous calling in—center on four vital areas of concern:

- Will the real Christians please stand up?
- Stop making idols of your institutions, buildings, rules, and dogma
- Go meet the God who is waiting outside
- Form loving, embodied communities that welcome our whole, authentic selves

Do I believe these "prophetic" Nones and Dones have it all figured out? I do not. In fact, the folk with whom I spoke were quick to admit how difficult they find it to form authentic community, how technology corrodes social connection and self-esteem, and how thin spiritual life can become when it's void of any authority beyond the self. The Millennial zeitgeist with its rampant self-centeredness, anti-institutionalism, and consumerism can veer toward anti-social and anti-human in a heartbeat. The bulk of younger Americans desperately seek supportive relationships and structures, even if they balk at the doorway to traditional institutions.

So no, they don't have all the answers, but I remain convinced God continues to walk with them and is speaking to us through them. It's worth the effort to receive and wrestle with their prophecy; the challenge and guidance that follows could spur churches to adapt and thrive in the decades ahead. The bonus: More Millennials and Gen Zers might eventually join us, especially if we saw them less as projects and more as partners, if we got intentional about removing the barriers to authentic belonging, and if we were willing to take more risks in order to look and love more like Jesus.

Rest assured, I also believe churches bring gifts and treasures aplenty to this two-way conversation. In Part IV you'll see a host of ways faith communities and institutions can respond to the prophecy of Nones and Dones and embrace faith in the future. In this moment, as you prepare to read and receive the prophecies, I hope you'll set aside the need for answers and next steps. Instead, let's lean into these four specific, spiritual capacities . . .

Cultivate Curiosity

Carve out mental and heart space to truly hear others and be curious about what God will do next.

An abiding, non-self-centered curiosity is essential for every disciple. Why? Because God is always up to something new. That's the promise in Isaiah 43:

> Remember not the former things,
>   nor consider the things of old.
> Behold, I am doing a new thing;
>   now it springs forth, do you not perceive it? (vv. 18–19)

Can we perceive it? We won't if we fixate on our desires and preferences or on the past. True, God's activity and words to prior generations are to be treasured, but our call in this day is to carry those gifts and wisdom forward. We are the ones entrusted with God's promise to bear something new in this world. God needs us to be curious enough to listen, to perceive what God is doing, and to discern in community what parts we can play.

As you take in the prophecies, notice moments when you feel defensive, misunderstood, or like you want to argue a point. Is there an aspect of truth here, given the speakers' experiences? What awareness might God be growing in you as you listen to a new and perhaps less complimentary perspective? Have you ever been surprised by the wisdom or story of someone quite different from you? How could you develop the capacity for curiosity in yourself and others?

Together, we can allow the walls to come down and welcome curiosity to rise.

Cultivate Humility

Admit we don't have all the answers,
and sometimes we've gotten it wrong.

In Mark 6, we see Jesus coming off a winning streak. He had healed a woman who suffered hemorrhaging for 12 years, and he followed up by raising Jairus's daughter from the dead. But when he tried teaching in the synagogue in his hometown, people whispered, "Is not this the carpenter, the son of Mary and brother of James and Joses and Judas and Simon, and are not his sisters here with us?" His power sputtered out (Mark 6:2–5).

Jesus wasn't always on. You and I won't be either. We're bound to face situations where our best efforts are simply not enough. Our gifts don't fit the context. The tried-and-true strategies don't work anymore. And sometimes, we simply get it wrong.

As you reflect with the prophecies and what may feel like criticism, draw on your inner reserve of humility. Wonder about times when you messed up and discovered power in that vulnerability. Have you ever met the limit of your abilities and had to "let go and let God"? What made it possible? How did you approach failure after that? How could you develop the capacity for humility in yourself and others?

Remember: at some point we've all fallen short, all hurt someone, all had the right intentions and still witnessed the wrong outcomes. The only difference is whether we can humbly call on God's power to perfect our weakness and make things whole.

Cultivate Mutuality

Go to accompany and learn from others
and welcome them to accompany and learn from us.

When Jesus dispatched the 72 disciples to go to all the towns he hoped to visit, he told them not to carry a purse, bag or sandals, but to receive the hospitality of those who know the place better (Luke 10:4, 10:7–8). Why wouldn't they bring all their best goods and establish mastery early on? He knew they needed to get rooted and real with a community, share life with them as he shared it with us, and eventually trust the host community's wisdom and gifts. Only then would a reconciled vision be possible, one where both groups weave a quilt more beautiful than either could craft on their own.

The Evangelical Lutheran Church in America calls this the ministry of accompaniment—"a walking together that practices interdependence and mutuality"—and it shapes their engagement with people globally and locally.[1] Instead of me carrying the gospel across to you, accompaniment assumes God's story is already present everywhere, including in your midst. My role is to walk alongside, to learn from and with you, to share what God has given me *and* discover together how God might call us both to be part of what God wants to do next for the sake of love.

I've spent most of my ministry helping churches and denominational bodies to embrace mutuality and transformation like this. What the Lutherans call accompaniment, I've understood as radical welcome: embracing the gifts, voices, power, and presence of groups traditionally on the margins, so that those inside and those outside might be healed and transformed, and we all taste more of the fullness of God.[2] A key insight is that the more powerful partner may need to be vulnerable first, may need to cross over to issue the invitation into relationship, and may need to proactively make room for the gift and voice of The Other. That is the opportunity before our churches now.

As you imagine walking with Millennial and Gen Z Nones and Dones in your life, allow yourself to recall a moment when you showed up to help someone, only to discover you needed their help. Maybe the gift they really needed you to share wasn't a strength you value. Or have you ever thought you had the answers and instead needed someone else's wisdom, especially someone you originally thought had little to offer?

The goal is not for one group to win and another to lose. It's not for one group to be right and the other to be wrong. It's about all of us discovering how God's story has been unfolding in our respective circles, and understanding the whole story is more holy and compelling when we tell it together.

Cultivate Love

Believe you are beloved, and that there is enough love to go around.

Jesus's public ministry didn't start with a big speech in the temple. That moment would come, but first, he went to the Jordan to be baptized. "Just as he was coming up out of the water, he saw the heavens torn apart and the Spirit descending like a dove on him. And a voice came from the heavens, 'You are my Son, the Beloved; with you I am well pleased'" (Mark 1:10–11). In other words, before he set out to love and save the world, Jesus needed to be filled with the unequivocal knowledge of his own belovedness. If anything, I am persuaded that Jesus's saturation in his Abba God's love is what made it possible for him to go out and love the world as he did.

When troubles come, God's love remains. When the membership seems sparse, God's Spirit won't leave you. When people travel alternate spiritual pathways that don't lead to your door, it's not a sign that God has abandoned you. With power and belovedness running through your veins, you can be generous and daring in offering welcome and respect to others. You can meet the young Nones and Dones in your own community and life, and you can embrace huge adaptive challenges, all because you are wrapped in the love of the One who made the world.

As you reflect on the urgent words in the next chapters, you may feel rejected—they don't want us, so why should we listen to them? You may feel competitive—we've only got a tiny piece of the religious pie, so we better defend it. Return to the truth that we are all beloved by God and all useful to God. What would you do if you knew God's love won't leave you? What would you risk, what would you love, who would you partner with, and what could you help to grow, if you were that free?

Opening our hearts, ears, and minds to the unexpected prophecy of young Nones and Dones could also open us to receive the breath and spirit that our loving God longs to pour into the church's dry bones.

Will the Real Christians Please Stand Up?
(First Prophecy)

Effie is looking for peace and protection in a troubled world. From what she can see, the church doesn't care. She's twenty-one, Asian-White, and was raised in Missouri in a conservative Christian family with rules so restrictive she had to move out as soon as possible. Now she's a self-supporting student in Minnesota. I met her on break at the popular coffee shop where she works, and she was breathtakingly honest.

"I don't mean to politicize this, but what's happening right now in our country under Trump, it makes me emotional," she said. "America is in a tough place. I'm scrolling my phone, and it's hard to look away. It makes me more spiritual because I sense so much evil with what's happening in our country. I have the urge to find peace now more than ever."

Would she look to churches for that solace? Probably not. When she sees organized religion, she doesn't see institutions that share her heart. She said they seem to be guarding their million- and even billion-dollar endowments rather than investing significantly in addressing a suffering world.

She is also tired of churches and religious groups attempting to soft-pedal social justice and maintain neutrality in order to hold people with disparate ideologies together. She's not sure that's where Jesus would be right now. "If you're not actively doing something to help, it's not neutral," she said. "There is no neutral in this moment. You're either helping or you're not. So take a firm stance on the side of people of color, trans people, the LGBTQ community, immigrants. You need to be actively supporting those communities and very clear about it."

Then she shrugged her shoulders. "But I understand some communities are really content with the current state and hate."

Effie's words and disappointment have lingered in my ears and on my heart. She and so many Nones and Dones view the church as an institution content with the status quo—even as the state powers actively target and wound the most vulnerable among us. Some of them left churches tainted by White Christo-nationalism. Others are disillusioned with moderate and liberal Christians and what they see as a relatively soft commitment to Jesus and his way of love.

Basil is a college student in New York now, but they grew up in a small evangelical church in Arkansas. Basil's home church took a hard right turn and became more anti-LGBTQ just as they were coming into their own queer identity; since then they've been in the wilderness. A few years ago, Basil heard a podcast where two evangelical YouTube personalities disclosed their own struggle toward freedom. That example was inspiring.

"These guys Brett and Link hosted a show back in the day called 'Good Mythical Morning,'" Basil told me. "I've watched it since I was a kid. Later they had this podcast called 'Ear Biscuits.' At the beginning of 2020, they released a deconstruction episode where they revealed that they were no longer Christian."

It was a huge moment for Basil, who was at the same time reconsidering their own relationship with the church.

> During one of the podcast episodes, I remember Brett saying, "Gen Z people are not leaving the church because you didn't teach them well enough. They're leaving the church because you taught them too well. You taught them what Jesus said about helping people, about standing with the poor, with minorities. They listened to that, and they internalized that. And then you turned around and you didn't do that." When he said that, I felt it. When you hear the church preach love, but then they don't do the things that align with what you know love is, it's obvious. And it's painful.

If more progressively minded churches think the alienation Basil described is a problem only for conservative evangelicals, they're wrong. Rebecca is twenty-four, White, and grew up in an Episcopal Church in Pennsylvania (her mom was the priest). She now lives with her husband in Virginia. After I saw her January 2025 blog post titled "Why Don't Young Adults Go to Church Anymore?,"[1] I knew we had to talk. Here's what she wrote in that letter to mainline churches:

> We were raised as good Christians. We went to church and Sunday school and CCD for our Catholic friends. And often,

our parents modeled church as something you go to because you had to prove to everyone else that you were a good person (turns out the need to prove yourself to everyone around you isn't unique to our generation). It's something we did because we were told to do it, and nobody ever really explained what value it was meant to add to our lives—just like the generations that came before us.

But we sat in those hard wooden pews while the adults read the Gospels and sang the psalms and loudly glared at us if we did something to affront them—like fidget. And something happened that I'm not sure our elders saw coming—we listened. We listened to the teachings of Jesus of Nazareth, a non-White refugee from the Middle East who was executed by the Roman state because he was too disruptive of their institutional norms.

We listened to the stories of the prophets like Job who constantly wrestled with God. We recited the Lord's Prayer and the Nicene Creed and acknowledged we are deeply imperfect people in service of a perfectly adoring God—and the highest value we can add to our lives and the lives of others is by loving one another as Christ loved us, and to do all things in the remembrance of him.

Then we came into the church in our adult lives. And instead of being welcomed into a respite from a world that demands more and more from us and finding the love Jesus preached, church welcomes us into institutional maintenance.

Again and again, I heard from young Nones and Dones like Rebecca who wanted to follow Jesus. They just weren't willing to prop up self-centered institutions or to hurt others in his name, two practices they clearly associate with traditional religion.

Victor took his inclusive church seriously when they said, "All are welcome!" He noticed they always had food left after their sumptuous coffee hour, so he decided it was time to share. "I brought in homeless people to one of our Sunday lunches," he said. "I mean, we had so much extra food, and I was tired of walking it out to them, so I just told them to come in. And a member gave me a very polite talking-to later about doing that."

He said the experience taught him the difference between preaching compassion and actively offering it, especially if the act of kindness makes church life uncomfortable. "It really opened my eyes that some people might be Christians, and they might have similar values to you, but they're afraid."

These revelations all track with research The Episcopal Church commissioned in 2021 for the "Jesus in America" survey.[2] Among other things, we wanted to know what people thought of Jesus and what they made of his church. The results were great for Jesus:

- Nearly 85 percent of Americans think Jesus is a significant spiritual leader, and three in four think he actually lived (as opposed to calling him a mythical figure).
- Americans identified Jesus's top teachings as follows:
  –Love your neighbor
  –Love God
  –Don't judge others without first judging yourself

The feedback shifted dramatically when people were asked about Christians:

- One in four Americans said Christians do not represent the values and teachings of Jesus. More than half of nonreligious people reported they don't see Jesus when they look at us.
- Christians most often described ourselves using the words "giving," "compassionate," "loving," and "respectful."
- Non-Christians most often described Christians with these words: "hypocrisy," "judgmental," "self-righteousness," and "arrogance."

Americans overall don't have a problem with Jesus, unless they're being forced to pray or pledge devotion to him. Their problem is with Christians. As Caroline in New York explained: "My friends who are not religious think every religious person is a bigot. I don't think that's true, but that is a very common conception."

Why did that idea surface? At least half of my partners named the Religious Right's bigotry and control of the Christian narrative as a reason why they sought distance from Christianity. Even among Nones and Dones who grew up in a positive, inclusive religious community, they struggle now to associate with a tradition that's so publicly allied with exclusion, judgment, patriarchy, and homophobia.

It's important to note: They're not necessarily happy about losing their religion. Mark Scandrette lives in San Francisco and serves as spiritual counsel to a number of nonreligious people. He once visited a tattoo artist at work and ended up chatting with a guest in the studio.

"This dude told me, 'Jesus is cool, but you Christians just fucked with Jesus.'" Mark laughed as only someone who has been in the trenches between the church and the nonreligious can. "He told me Christianity was at its best when it was this secret, hidden movement characterized by love. But he said what I felt: We fucked with Jesus."

Mark and his conversation partner found a colorful way to express a truth we've all witnessed: Many Christians and Christian institutions claim the name of Jesus but don't follow his gospel teachings. If anything, they use his name to justify actions Jesus himself would have vehemently opposed: hurting the poor, immigrants, children, vulnerable women, nondominant cultures, and sexual minorities; congratulating and coddling the wealthy; and pursuing personal prosperity at others' expense. Many of the Nones and Dones I met were genuinely furious about White Christo-nationalism[iii] and the abuse of Jesus's name and wondered why true Christians haven't been more vocal in reclaiming Jesus's mission.

Key in Minnesota was booted from her family church a few years ago for bringing her girlfriend to worship. She eventually left the church, but she knew Jesus wouldn't have affirmed the way she was treated. "God didn't sit with the rich and wealthy and live with them and focus on them," she said. "He sat with the poor. He would have sat with the gypsies, the gays, the

---

iii As I explained in Chapter 1, I do not use the phrase "White Christian Nationalism." I prefer to speak of "White Christo-nationalism," and thus to separate Jesus and true Christianity from the heresy of church and political leaders who combine Christian symbols and language with greed, hate, and authoritarianism.

adulterers. So if you're going to live and dedicate your life to him, then be careful you do it the way he would have."

A cradle Roman Catholic with strong social justice leanings, Kelly in Minnesota was certain Jesus would not compromise the truth in order to keep favored status with the government, something she sees churches doing regularly. "I know it's a hard one—I write grants for nonprofits!—but at some point, your 501(c)(3) certification be damned," she said. "When something is wrong, call it wrong. In a lot of churches I've been to, there's no preaching on that. Nothing. They're silent."

When Christians finally speak and sound like Jesus, it's music to the Nones and Dones' ears. Ashley is an atheist in Clarksville, Tennessee, but still cheered as The Right Reverend Mariann Budde, Bishop of the Episcopal Diocese of Washington, preached about compassion and mercy during the January 2025 presidential inaugural prayer service. At last, Ashley said, here was a Christian leaning into the fullness of Jesus's teaching.

> We don't have a foundational text for atheism, but Christians have a book they follow that literally says, you've got to take care of people and don't step on the weak. So you can stand up in church in front of Trump and tell him that he's not following the principles that he purports to stand for. I don't have a book like that, but you do. You have words that say you shouldn't let people freeze to death outside or get steamrolled for living in homeless encampments. So speak them!

Stepping up in these ways might cost Christians and our institutions. We might seem radical and noncooperative to the powers our churches once befriended. Some members might depart if they think their churches have become too "political." I wish they could hear Effie's comment that churches seem quiet and "content with the current state and hate." Nones and Dones are terrified of the White Christo-nationalist takeover of Jesus's movement. They want to know if actual Christians are scared, too.

Stop Making Idols of Your Institutions, Buildings, Rules, and Dogma

(Second Prophecy)

Micah sat down recently to read the prophet Jeremiah. Mind you, the Micah I spoke with is not the late biblical prophet; he's a 24-year-old, religiously unaffiliated theology student currently based in Atlanta. Sometimes God leads him to open Scripture and read. This time, it was Jeremiah 24, where the prophet addresses the Israelites exiled in Babylon and tells them about two baskets of figs. One basket is good, representing the Israelites who are ready to return to God and understand they will undergo great change; the other basket contains rotten figs, like the Israelites who are unwilling to change.

Micah said he heard a divine word to the church in this passage:

> The message for the church from this text is, change or die. Yes, change hurts. Change is being carried away captive, losing everything that has created your identity in the land. But remaining the same is death. So change is going to hurt, but that's the only way you'll return to God. It might not look the same as it did before. It's still the only way.

If there's anything the dozens of Nones and Dones I met agree on, it's this: Churches too often foster rigid attitudes toward belief, structure, labels, and/or practice, and they need to learn to change or prepare to die. This isn't a personal judgment. As Micah explained, all living things change, especially if they're in relationship with a living God. "That's what the church is facing right now," he said. "Change or die."

Benjamin is twenty-five and lives in New York. He shares Micah's conviction that institutions need to change, but he's not waiting for that day. "It'd be cool if old institutions tuned in to the subtleties of spiritual guidance in a different way and were able to help facilitate transformation on the planet," he said. "And if they don't, okay. It'll happen some other way."

He told me he wasn't being dismissive, only practical and honest. "There's this seed in my heart that says, 'We're all intrinsically connected,' so we will evolve and wake up at whatever pace we can," he explained. "I am excited for a day when people with power, resource, and agency get penetrated by insight." He has genuine hope that religious institutions will at last wake and put the Spirit first.

Rebecca is eager to see that change, and she told me she wrote her January blog post about young adults abandoning church as a "letter to organized religion."[1] She knows churches are human institutions, so they're going to get some things right and some things wrong (she actually attends church on a regular basis but describes herself as "vaguely spiritual with strong uncertainty"). At this stage, she said, Christian institutions have traveled too far from their purpose. The current systemic decline could serve as a necessary if purging corrective.

> The church institution is dying. I say let it. The institutional church has become far too concerned with its self-preservation, to the detriment of its pursuit of Jesus and service of God. Let us get back to our Christian roots. Let us stop worrying about buildings but instead concern ourselves with meeting people where they are to share the good news. Let us stop asking how we can make our community come to us but instead ask how we can enrich our communities.

Rebecca was far from alone in her frustration around the idolatry of church buildings. A few people pointed to megachurch leader Joel Osteen, whose Houston church did not initially provide shelter to Hurricane Harvey victims in 2017, even though the church owns the city's former pro basketball coliseum. Setting aside that extreme example, and even acknowledging the beauty and history of religious architecture and its capacity to draw people closer to the divine, my partners were generally mystified about why churches continue to invest such a huge proportion of their time, money, and heart into their buildings and structures.

Casper in New York regularly consults with faith organizations, so even though he's not religious, he has wrestled plenty with this issue. "The whole question of buildings is fraught, because there are so many lovely places," he said. "But honestly—the amount of money and energy that gets spent. If you didn't have to do so much of that, I imagine it would be clearer what the church's job is."

In addition to tying up money and energy that could better serve direct mission, Casper wondered if the building obsession is part of our nostalgia for the glory days of Christian establishment. "Those buildings are like a representation of respectability, power, and influence, even though churches don't really have that anymore," he said. "You have a lot to offer, but it's just probably not in the way you think."

Beyond the loaded issues surrounding our buildings, these young Nones and Dones were deeply concerned about rigid approaches to rules and faith statements. The way they see it—and many people of faith would agree—no human words or formulas could ever fully capture the nature of God, so churches should hold our doctrine more lightly and humbly.

Melia agrees, and she is actually quite religious. Her dad is the head of Grace Cathedral in San Francisco, and she led the Episcopal student group in her days at Yale University. But when she takes nonreligious friends to church, she knows what to expect. "One of my best friends said, 'I love Grace Cathedral. I would totally go again. But the part I really hated was when everyone stood up and started chanting their beliefs.'"

At first I didn't know what Melia's friend was referencing. Melia spelled it out.

> My friend was talking about the Creed. And I thought, "I don't know if I really believe some of those things, but it's nice to stand with everyone and say together, 'We believe in God,

> the Father, and maker of heaven and earth.'" But now that I look back, I can totally see how she thought, "Whoa!" It was totally open and welcoming, and then there's this chorus of the whole group saying words that most regular people don't even understand.

Melia's friend's response is a common one among nonreligious people when they think about faith communities. According to the Pew Research Center, a high proportion of Nones cite disagreement with doctrine as the number one reason they aren't religious. They might not be asking us to dismiss the basic tenets of the faith, but could we reconsider how we share them? In that public moment of stating the Creed, people with doubts and questions like Melia's friend often feel they can only participate if they sign off on an incomprehensible credal statement in its entirety. That's a tall order, especially for younger generations who've been trained to question institutions and labels.

Arpan teaches high schoolers in Atlanta, and he gently suggested faith communities might borrow the wisdom of the classroom and introduce a more gracious, spacious approach to faith. "I wonder if religious institutions could try something like project-based learning," he offered. "Instead of giving a kid a test and having only one right answer, if you really want to see their knowledge and creativity, give them a rubric. As long as they meet certain criteria, it doesn't matter how they present it."

He then transferred that lesson to churches. "So the institution can have its core beliefs, but create an environment where individuals, especially young individuals, are allowed to be more comfortable and at ease expressing whatever feelings, doubts, and questions they have. And it's all right because we've all gathered as a community to help each other to reach our potential."

Like Arpan, most of the Nones and Dones I met are realistic about the need for some structure and infrastructure, and some have even become champions for healthy institutions. Take Alex, who offered this wise perspective: "We can't abandon institutions. Honestly, they can do things at scale that individuals or small communities cannot. And we don't have time to remake the world. We need these places. And frankly, saying my own life and experience is the only authority I can trust is exhausting."

Where does that leave us? Certainly not without any institutions, beliefs, buildings, or structures at all, but perhaps with a more nuanced approach, one that encourages churches to discern what God's mission requires us to keep and to release. Churches have historically leaned into maintenance and preservation. Our nonreligious friends remind us that now it's time to cross-train for flexibility, generosity, and letting go.

Go Meet the God Who Is Waiting Outside
(Third Prophecy)

When Ezekiel and the Israelites were banished to Babylon, he thought his life with God was over. God had a surprise in store: The Spirit met him on the banks of the Chaldea River and gave him a vision. My conversation partners shared story after story of their own vivid encounters with God outside religious buildings and structures, most often in the great outdoors. Their prophecy back to the church: Go meet God in nature; in the earthly, dark, and feminine; and in our everyday lives.

Mystics have offered this guidance for centuries and been met with the church's disapproval. Fourteenth-century German Catholic priest Meister Eckhart was named a heretic in his day, in part for statements like this: "Apprehend God in all things, for God is in all things. Every single creature is full of God and a book about God. Every creature is a word of God. If I spent enough time with the tiniest creature—even a caterpillar—I would never have to prepare a sermon. So full of God is every creature."[1]

Especially as the human mark on the world looks more and more like a stain, people need to commune with a creative power greater than humanity. College student Irina, twenty-one, longs for just that kind of experience. "I feel a disenchantment with the world we've made," she said. "Things feel really dark. Being in nature feels like a relief because there's this thing that I don't understand, that no one could make, but it just is."

Kimberley in Philadelphia didn't grow up seeking God's presence in nature, but that changed amidst the isolation of the pandemic. "During COVID, I had a class that encouraged me to meditate out in nature," she told me. "I had so many rich communion experiences with the divine, almost as rich as times I'd previously 'caught the Holy Spirit' in church services. Since then, hiking and meditating by the water have become really important to me in my spiritual practice."

Julianna also accesses God in nature, but she has been hesitant to name it because she is still part of a Christian community (though labels make her nervous). As the White, 40-year-old mother of two in Atlanta explained: "Going back to nature, the ability to observe creation, to connect with something outside myself, it supports health, well-being, and mental capacity in a different way than sitting inside listening to a sermon. That's sometimes less relatable and doesn't resonate with my own life."

The prophetic word these Nones and Dones speak is a simple one: If we know God meets us, speaks to us, and heals us outside of church, especially in nature but also in ordinary life, why doesn't the church honor and prioritize these outside meetings with God? The reasons are legion. Maybe because churches can't control those experiences and stories. Or because people might have more transformative, empowering, revelatory encounters outside than inside and start to wonder why they come into church at all. Maybe because the church has traditionally been fueled by masculine "God the Father" energy that dominates the earth and the feminine.

All these arguments ring true for Gael, who is gender nonbinary, remains on the fringe of their San Francisco Catholic community, and has practiced earth-centered traditions since they were young.

> I don't know if it's my queerness. I don't know if it's my femininity. But somewhere around the age of twelve, I started turning for answers towards the earth. The Catholic Church—especially the one I grew up in—is the epitome of masculinity. So I needed to draw towards Mother Nature, towards the earth, towards looking inside my own power, which is not exclusively masculine.

Morgan in Massachusetts is also eager to liberate the notion of the sacred from controlling, masculine paradigms. As a teen, she ran from images of a terrifying, punishing God. Now she understands the Spirit is bigger than what she was taught.

> I experience the sacred every day. I have a dog—I'm petting him as I'm sitting here talking to you—and I experience a sacred connection to this animal because he is a being that I love deeply. I experience the sacred when I happen to wake up in time to see the sunrise and take him on a walk around the reservoir. Every time I smile at someone else when I'm passing them on the street, it's sacred: It's a human connection, animal connection, a recognition of our shared place on this earth.

My partners also encouraged churches to reach beyond their walls and embrace the diverse cultures and practices around them. That's no surprise, given that Millennials and Gen Z together make up the two most racially diverse generations in American history. Interracial dating, work, and socializing are increasingly a given for this cohort, and many of them have clear convictions against aligning with racist organizations. Imagine what it's like for them walking into our churches, most of which tend to be mono-racial and/or mono-cultural.

Kimberley was frustrated that she had to choose between a progressive church that matched her values but didn't adequately welcome her as a Black woman, or a more theologically conservative church that mirrored the racial diversity of her community. For a time, she went with the conservative but diverse option.

"I migrated to multicultural, non-denominational churches for a while," she said. "I feel strongly that heaven wouldn't be segregated, whatever life is waiting after this one. And I feel very strongly about multicultural work for the kingdom of God in our everyday practical reality."

Eventually, she said she had to leave that integrated church because she couldn't compromise on gospel values like love and welcome for all God's people. Now that she's an interfaith hospital chaplain, she said she is free to celebrate God's presence in all people and places.

Young Nones and Dones are urging churches to step out and wake up to what God is doing in the world. They're inviting us to honor the sacred in nature, in everyday life, and in diverse settings. And they're asking us to bless and incorporate those experiences into our ritual and shared life.

Form Loving, Embodied Communities That Welcome Our Whole, Authentic Selves

(Fourth Prophecy)

At the climax of Ezekiel's prophetic encounter in the valley of the dry bones, God issues this command:

> Prophesy to these bones and say to them: O dry bones, hear the word of the Lord! Thus says the Lord God to these bones: I will cause breath to enter you, and you shall live. I will lay sinews on you and will cause flesh to come upon you and cover you with skin and put breath in you, and you shall live, and you shall know that I am the Lord (Ezekiel 37:4–6).

The Nones and Dones I met announced a similar prophecy to the church's dry bones. They're calling us to be incarnate and enfleshed, to be authentic and real, to be fully and passionately alive, and to act like we love and trust one another.

The Incarnation of Jesus may be a core tenet for Christian communities, but my conversation partners didn't see us embracing it nearly often enough. I asked Stephanie in San Francisco what she'd tell the churches, and she didn't hesitate: "I think they all need to dance more!" She communicates with the divine through her body—whether she's dancing, doing yoga, or engaged in walking meditation—and believes the church should trust the unpredictable wisdom of our bodies and life experiences.

> God shows up in so many ways outside of the rigidity that I saw growing up [in an evangelical central California community]. There was a lot of fear. There was obligation. There was only one way of doing things. And obviously, religion or God or spirituality cannot be contained. Let it loosen up, and let kids be kids, and encourage all the people to find God in places that might surprise them.

My partners invited us to imagine a church where people gather and experience freedom, authenticity, and genuine community. Jax grew up attending an Episcopal Church in New York. He said he actually felt connected to people and knew he was loved. He just wished that spirit had infused and loosened up the worship.

> The church tells us, in order to see this community that you like, you have to sit through an hour of just listening to people talk. I keep thinking the service itself should be community,

> but it's just monotonous: I promise to do this, I know this, and I understand that God did this, and all of that. Why can't they make the actual service feel more like a community?

More than a critique of worship, Jax is returning to wisdom we heard in the chapters about the sacred and belonging: Community is a sacrament, for God is revealed and known in the very space between us. Church professionals often focus on preaching, baptism, and the communion table, in part because that's where the institution asked us to hone our expertise. These Nones and Dones remind us what Trinitarian theology should've taught us all along: Our God is a God of relationship, and we know God and practice God's ways when we are in relationship.

That said, Jax isn't necessarily wrong about worship, which can indeed be a dry experience. Flor in Atlanta said she has struggled with church worship, starting with the basics. "A lot of what's hard is just the church format, which is pretty hard to change," she said. "An hour is a long time to be in the building, just sitting there. And in the South, it's a more formal occasion. If I'm not dressed up, I feel a little bad."

She wasn't criticizing the church's culture or preference. "That's the church's character, and it's allowed to have that," she said. "But it's not paying attention to a whole generation. We're out here saying, 'Well that's fine for you but not for us.'"

Flor is right: Several of my conversation partners said either they or their friends couldn't imagine sitting and listening to a standard twelve- to twenty-minute sermon. They're used to short, compelling TikTok videos. They're also accustomed to opportunities to talk back in the chat or comments section. Silent, passive reception of one clergyperson's word as authoritative is downright weird.

And when younger generations finally sit and listen, they often can't understand our words. Let's admit that religious language frequently sounds nothing like the words regular people speak to one another. It's elevated, churchy, and often inaccessible. While that might appeal to some cultures or generations—and some young people might enjoy the history, poetry, and formality—it is a foreign tongue to most Millennials and Gen Zers and to nonreligious people as a whole. When we double-down and cling to traditional church language, we should be aware that we're sending a dismissive message: You and your culture don't matter enough for us to adapt or translate in order to welcome you.

Andy said he feels intimidated by church worship, and he *works* at a church-based program in San Francisco. Still, he admitted to me:

> Church can give off a vibe. I went through a Salvation Army recovery program, and they gave us a Bible. Now, I'm a reader, so I tried probably ten times to read the Bible. And the language was so old. I don't know how else to describe it. A lot of the language is so out of date, it puts up a barrier, especially if you're not sure what you want in life. They need to explain in a way that's much more relatable and has to deal with today's life.

He said he's grateful for Father Kevin Deal, whose church hosts his organization and with whom he enjoys side chats about deep topics. Too often, my conversation partners told me church leaders didn't model how to be real and didn't bring their own authentic selves and stories to church. You could belong, but only if you put on the face, the clothes, and the show. That's what Craig in Minnesota witnessed throughout his childhood.

> I learned in the church that you don't talk about your problems or what's going on at home. But if this is your community, you should be able to tell people what's happening. They're supposed to be your biggest supporters. For me, open communication is key, and it starts with the preacher. Be vulnerable. Be real. The authenticity of communication with your congregation is what really brings the whole community closer.

Speaking up about what's happening in people's real lives makes a difference. Kelly in Minnesota tried attending church and never broke through. She said the leaders didn't connect to the community's actual hurts and hopes.

> We are not middle class by any stretch of the imagination. Things are very hard for people right now. The world just feels a little bit shittier and a little bit angrier every year. It is hard to give a crap about dogma or adopting a new tenet or whatever, when I can't afford groceries, when your church doesn't support my husband's union going on strike in a real way. What are you doing?

Liam in New York wants to know the same thing. When I asked what he would tell the churches, he unleashed genuine disappointment and frustration with the generations now running the church and nation:

> We are a generation with perpetual existential anxiety. We can see and hear the world around us. We're currently in the midst of a climate catastrophe that, if it's not solved, we're all dead. And we're going to be the generation that feels that the most acutely first. We understand what the stakes are. We are in a country that looked at school shootings becoming more and more routine. And as opposed to doing something to take away the things that are killing us, the government protected the thing that was killing us.
>
> Forgive my French, but we are fucking scared, and we're fucking scared all the time. And institutions, whether they be religious, whether they be state or worldwide, they would do well to understand that, and to work directly with us, as opposed to just writing off a Gen Z concern as us overreacting.

Nones and Dones are desperate to see churches and leaders finally addressing people's incarnate struggles. In the absence of real talk from real people in touch with the real world, many Millennial and Gen Z Nones and Dones said church just seems fake and useless. As Shannon Kelly has learned in her decades working with young adults, including a term as The Episcopal Church's lead on young adult and campus ministry, nothing damns us more than appearing inauthentic.

"There's no room for the fake or the easy answer," she explained. "They want to really delve in and show up and have conversations and talk across differences. And if we're not willing to do that, or if we're inauthentic about it, they see right through it, and they're not interested."

David spent decades in big-church ministry before he shifted to playing music at the Minneapolis/St. Paul airport. He tasted the fakeness Shannon warned about and finally got free. He may not identify with religious institutions anymore, but he really wants to see them change. His message was simple and urgent:

> Don't miss the boat. People need us every day, and we're not there for them. Until you find ways to really be there for people, you can't impact them just inside your walls and cubicles doing your work or even in your worship. They need to speak, become part of the services. They need to participate. When we lose that, and it's all about the professional people up front, that's when we lose a lot of the church.

David and other Nones and Dones welcome the day when more churches foster true community and make room for people to bring our authentic and embodied selves all the way inside. The days of getting by with passive, fake, obligatory participation are gone, and that should be good news for us all.

Nones and Dones may not be asking to directly participate in the church's life (though some are). Still, it behooves us to listen with a spirit of curiosity, humility, mutuality, and love. Practically speaking, they are a rising majority: 46 percent of Gen Z now identify as nonreligious, while 38 percent say they're Christian, and experts report Americans tend to become less religious as they age, so . . . do the math.

Apart from the numbers, we should listen because they are our peers, our children, our neighbors, our classmates. They are partners who share a fervent hope to heal this nation and world. They are encountering and embracing the sacred in unique ways. They are struggling to find authentic community where they can discover more meaning, purpose, and love. And it appears God has given them a vision those of us on the inside can't see with the same clarity. What we do with that prophetic offering—and whether we continue in life-giving conversation with them—is ultimately up to us.

PART IV

THE FUTURE OF FAITH

If there is any hope for the future—and I believe there is—churches will need to walk humbly but boldly in our increasingly post-Christian landscape, make room for the insights and leadership of generations for whom this culture is home, and together reimagine how to embody the way of Jesus for our time. We can't just sit around meditating on our failures or waiting for a new generation to fall in love with our beloved treasures. We've got to step into the future.

I hope you feel the presence of new friends gathered around to share this journey. If your church intends to cooperate with God and rise from the valley, you will find so many Nones and Dones ready to cheer you on. Some you've heard throughout this book. Others are in your life already, just waiting for a conversation (use the online Resource, Reflection, and Action Guide that accompanies this book and go to meet them!). The endgame is not to attract these nonreligious people (back) to church; nor is it to dump religion as you've known it and remake it to the liking of the Nones and Dones we've just met. Instead, in this section, I hope we can build a bridge. Our work is to listen to what God is saying within and beyond the churches, to accept God's invitation to change (instead of blaming Nones and Dones for not joining us), to discern the next faithful steps, and to get moving. *Now*.

No one could chart the path alone, and I hope you don't try. In fact, to write this section, I enlisted colleagues to join me in reflecting with the prophecies and imagining the future of faith. The insights that follow come from a collective, with especially helpful contributions from these colleagues:

- Dr. Courtney Cowart, who heads the Society for the Increase of Ministry, a scholarship-granting organization that fuels leadership formation and transformation
- Jerusalem Greer, co-executive director of the Procter Center, a camp and retreat center in Ohio (she's also an exvangelical, former Southern Baptist who headed The Episcopal Church's evangelism ministries for years)
- The Reverend Zack Nyein, senior associate at St. Bartholomew's Church in New York City and Pastor for Imagine Worship, a fresh expression of tradition within the existing church
- The Reverend Dr. Blair Pogue, canon for vitality and innovation in the Episcopal Church in Minnesota
- The Reverend Katie Nakamura Rengers, former lead on church planting and new ministry development for The Episcopal Church
- The Reverend Dr. Dwight Zscheile, professor of congregational mission and leadership at Luther Seminary in St. Paul, Minnesota

These generous leaders were by my side through much of the journey: combing through interview narratives, culling the prophecies, and discerning what all this could mean for the future of faith. I'm also grateful for the church leaders—many of them Millennials and Gen Zers—who spoke to me on the road about their ministries with young Nones and Dones. Together, they've helped me to picture a church that honors our heritage in the faith, respects the wisdom of the margins, and above all, heeds Jesus's invitation to become communities of love, freedom, and abundant life for all.

The Truth Before Us

You don't need the voices of Nones and Dones to tell you something's got to change in American Christian life. The facts are present in our pews and in the news. It may be helpful to revisit some of those truths now. Here's what we know:

The figures in Part I of this book tell the story of a Christianity that is less and less compelling to people of all generations, particularly younger ones. Religious decline and disaffiliation are especially pronounced among moderate and progressive Americans who have witnessed the rising domination of the Religious Right and White Christo-nationalism and fled affiliation with the label "Christian."

We know these two trends—the lack of generational replacement and the disappearance of non-conservative Christians—together explain a good chunk of the titanic decline of Protestant mainline churches over the last few decades. I am aware that several of those denominations now quietly speak of an expiration date—an actual point in this century when their numbers will have shrunk so much they will no longer be able to maintain a significant footprint in American life, regardless of the cash and property on hand.

We know that evangelicals thought they had dodged this fate, but now they're also seeing more liberal and young people (especially young women) joining the ranks of the "exvangelicals." We know recent surveys have indicated a temporary pause in Christianity's rapid decline, partly thanks to growth among Pentecostals and conservative, traditional religious expressions, including Catholicism. Some Americans crave their promise of certainty in an uncertain world; others have begun to tick the box for "Christian" because of the draw of White Christonationalism, which uses Christian symbols, language, and structures to advance a racist political agenda antithetical to the way of Jesus.

What else? We know the post-Christian cultural forces of privatization, secularization, and pluralization have all contributed to what scholars call the Age of Authenticity or the Millennial zeitgeist. In this technology- and media-saturated age, we're told our individual experience and authority hold the highest value, and the highest human pursuit is the perfection of our own mental, physical, emotional, and spiritual state. People are more isolated and lonely than ever, and less likely to join or trust the religious and civic bodies that once connected and grounded us in community.

We know the unbridled culture of consumption has infected the spiritual landscape, and all manner of religious products, methods, and messages can be packaged, rebranded, and sold. People of all ages now often stumble along an individualized path seeking meaning, hope, love, and the sacred, and younger generations who have been saturated in this culture say they are more lonely and unmoored than any group in American history.

But we also know Americans have a robust, almost weedlike instinct for spirituality—our longing persists despite all the forces trying to choke or control it. So the vast majority of us still report we believe in God or a higher power, at dramatically higher rates than our more secular counterparts across Europe. We still pray, often daily. Even among the approximately one-third of Americans who identify as "nonreligious"—the Nones and Dones—most say they're "nothing in particular" rather than claiming to be "agnostic" or "atheist." Many of us want community. We want the sacred. We're just unclear on how to access both in ways that are sustainable, authentic, and fulfilling.

How might churches respond to these realities and the prophecies we've heard from our None and Done siblings?

Option A: We could simply double down on our bread and butter. Tend the flock who love what we love and pray as we pray. Continue the online services we started during the pandemic. Work chiefly on better preaching, music, and children's programs. Cross our fingers hoping to receive a wave of people alienated from the evangelical and Catholic churches of their youth. Otherwise turn from the tidal wave on the horizon, spend down endowments, and avoid making a significant, proactive effort to embrace institutional and spiritual transformation from within.

I hope we don't, because even if those religious refugees come to our doors, they are seeking more than inclusivity and ancient tradition as we have always lived them. They yearn for vitality, authenticity, participation, and a life saturated with sacred awareness. If they arrive at traditional religious communities that have little interest in transformed life or in Jesus, they won't stay for long (nor should they).

Option B: Churches may surrender and become more or less secular community organizations. Give up our core beliefs. (One church leader told me recently, "In the future, we're going to have to downplay Jesus"—as if our savior is a marketing liability.) Become wellness centers without any explicitly Christian moorings or witness.

I resist this option because the way of Jesus is a life-giving, liberating way for a nation swallowed up in greed, selfishness, and sin. Humans can join hands to make the world better, but our hope ultimately rests in our triune God, who has not left the scene.

Option C: Or churches can acknowledge all that we now know and then discern a faithful way forward in partnership with emerging generations who harbor a deep instinct for spirituality, desperately yearn for community, and may welcome churches to walk alongside them as we together figure out how to advance the loving dream of God.

I believe this is the only faithful option. And I know the prophecies of Millennial and Gen Z Nones and Dones can help to point the way. They remind us that a faith following in the footsteps of a spirit-powered revolutionary should speak more boldly than the false prophets who have ruthlessly stolen the name "Christian" in our day. A faith with the cross, death, and resurrection of God at the center can surely overcome the fears that make us cling to our institutions and structures, so we at last take a risk for the sake of the gospel. A faith whose Lord walked the highways and byways, taught on the mountainside, and had no place to lay his head, can surely go outside and join God's people in love for creation. A faith centered on a young holy man from the margins can surely embrace generational turnover and honor the gifts, presence, and power of young people within and beyond the institution.

Let's dream that faith now, one prophetic response at a time . . .

We Are the Jesus Movement

(Response to the First Prophecy)

The majority of Millennial and Gen Z Nones and Dones I met believe Christianity has turned its back on empathy, justice, love, and truth. Even if they personally grew up in a more inclusive and thoughtful church. Even if they know the popular conservative version of Christianity is a heresy, and that White Christo-nationalism is a brazen, sinful misrepresentation of the way of Jesus. All that goodwill may remain in their memory banks, but they long ago stopped expecting professed Christians to be anything like Jesus. Their challenge to us in the First Prophecy: "Will the Real Christians Please Stand Up?"

Whatever the future is for this faith of ours, whatever the contours of tomorrow's church, we have no choice but to center a more public, vocal, and bold witness to the radical love of Jesus by people who preach and live it. Nothing else can or should survive.

Where would we even begin? Not by getting louder and more ruthless than the Religious Right and Christo-nationalists, but perhaps with clarity about what we say the church and Christianity even exist for. The Right may be wrong about a lot, but you'll never have to wonder what they're promising: personal salvation from hell, protection for the unborn, tightly structured gender relations for the household and society, heterosexual marriage for all, continued dominance for America and the West, and the solid assurance that God is on your side.

In contrast, from what I've witnessed, moderate and progressive Christian circles seem unsure and even unconvinced on the "value proposition" for being Christian. Are we social service groups? Are we justice organizations? Are we music and architecture appreciation societies? Mainline churches have by and large ceded Jesus and Christianity to our conservative counterparts. We too often apologize for being followers of Jesus, if we say his name at all. So when we do good works and stand with the oppressed, outsiders think we're just good people. They don't look and say, "Oh, that's a follower of Jesus." They often don't know we exist at all. We need a solid, compelling vision around which Christians who don't identify with the Religious Right can coalesce and rise up; otherwise, we risk drifting further toward obsolescence.

Become the Jesus Movement

One of the many reasons I loved working with former Presiding Bishop Michael Curry was his ability to put simple, clear words to beliefs most Christians share. During his entire nine-year term as head of The Episcopal Church, he never missed an opportunity to tell us we were "the Episcopal branch of the Jesus Movement." As I look around, I'm convinced that call is now more urgent and timely than ever for all Christians. Here's why:

- The Jesus Movement, as we described it, is "the ongoing community of people who center their lives on Jesus and follow him into loving, liberating, and life-giving relationship with God, each other and creation."[1] So who are Christians? We're the community of people who've been following Jesus and trying to live like him for more than two thousand years, and we're helping one another and anybody else to have a loving relationship with God, with our neighbors and with this precious earth. No jargon. No confusion. And it's all about love. That will preach.
- Digging deeper, we need a fierce, strategic emphasis on Jesus rather than a particular church. Most denominational distinctions mean very little to people outside that group's fold; when I became an Episcopalian, an uncle asked if I was now a "pescatarian" and thus only eating fish (I've saved that text message to keep me honest).

  Meanwhile, as we've noted, Jesus still inspires hope in the public square. People see what the Religious Right is up to, and they know in their gut that's not Jesus. It's definitely the church—we've given people too many reasons to believe the worst about the institution. But they know a message of repression, cruelty, and selfishness doesn't match Jesus. The more we identify with him, the more we will be aligned with a recognizable source of truth, hope, and love. People don't trust us. They trust Jesus. We should, too.
- "Movement" is the presumed opposite of "institution," and we know how Americans feel about institutions these days. As Bishop Curry often pointed out:

> Jesus did not establish an institution, though institutions can serve his cause. He did not organize a political party, though his teachings have a profound impact on politics. Jesus did not even found a religion. No, Jesus began a movement, fueled by his Spirit, a movement whose purpose was and is to change the face of the earth from the nightmare it often is into the dream that God intends.[2]

Keep in mind, the man who spoke these words was the head of an international denomination, a leader at the pinnacle of institutional life. Still he invited us to keep our eyes on the prize: not to shore up the institution for its own sake, but to serve the loving, liberating, life-giving movement of God. It's an important message for people inside and outside the church to hear, especially given rampant, often warranted distrust toward institutions.

"Movement" also conjures a picture of passionate efforts for liberation, including the Suffragette Movement, the Indian Independence Movement, the Civil Rights Movement, the Anti-Apartheid Movement, the Gay Rights Movement, and more. It suggests mobilization, organization, and transformation. We need all that and more to counter White Christo-nationalism, which represents an existential threat to Christian values, to vulnerable people, and to the planet. We should act like we're part of an actual movement, cultivating the wisdom of serpents and the innocence of doves as we work to root out the heretic scourge of Christo-nationalism. We should be organizing to restore Jesus to his rightful place at the center of the faith that bears his name.

Ultimately, there won't be a single, magic, compelling description of mainline Christianity we can all agree on and run with. Still, I wonder if inviting Christians to live as branches of the Jesus Movement—as I know some denominations have over the last few years—could spark a powerful shift in narrative and identity.

Get Clear on Jesus's Values and Proclaim the Message

Emerging generations of Nones and Dones are impatient with our hesitation to give voice to Jesus's radical love. Recall Effie, who suggested churches are quiet because they're actually "content" with hate and meanness. She isn't sure we care that the world is burning.

There are ways of making that message plain without alienating the bulk of mainline Christians. Episcopal Bishop Mariann Budde of the Diocese of Washington (D.C.) made headlines by simply preaching about God's mercy before President Donald Trump.[3] That viral moment occurred just a few days after my visits to San Francisco, Atlanta, and New York, and I was amazed at how many None and Done conversation partners texted me to ask, "Have you seen this?" and "Is she one of yours?" They also just wanted to write/shout: "That's what I'm talking about!" If you listen to her words, she stayed close to Scripture, Jesus, the Beatitudes, and incontrovertibly Christian values like humility, love, and unity. She didn't rail and call names. She presented the gospel with clarity and made a plea to live more like Jesus. And she has undoubtedly paid a price (chatter about "the sin of empathy" skyrocketed among conservatives after her sermon).

Not all preachers are willing to share that gentle yet prophetic word from the pulpit on a Sunday, but many of them do. To those brave souls, I say, "God bless you." I also have to ask, on behalf of my None and Done friends, how are we bringing that message to the wider public? Are we writing op-eds for our town newspapers? Are we showing up at school board meetings begging for mercy and truth in the name of God? Are we volunteering to accompany undocumented children to court when their parents have been disappeared? Are we providing sanctuary to student protesters hunted by the police or ICE? Are our institutions resourcing us and giving us cover for the work of advocacy and witness? Thank God for every Christian and church who can say yes to any of those queries. Where are the rest of us? Our silence is telling.

Some of my church colleagues report that they're torn about more boldly standing on Jesus Movement values, because they don't want to alienate members or neighbors in the body of Christ. I spoke recently to a gay priest friend who urged his congregation not to place a rainbow flag on the church sign. He told me he was worried about damaging his dialogue with the local Baptist pastor. I asked why he wasn't also worried about the wounded LGBTQIA+ Baptists who have never seen a church affirm their dignity or their ministries. Why have we so prioritized keeping peace within the body at the expense of the truth of the gospel and with little regard for relationship with people already rejected and left on the side of the road? Why aren't we willing to take a biblically based risk to protect the persecuted and name the sin of greed, selfishness, and oppression? Again, our silence is telling.

After conversation with so many younger Nones and Dones, I confess I am less willing to make these compromises than I was even months before I launched this listening project. I hear them asking me, as Craig did: "Are you walking in Jesus's footsteps? Because he walked next to the homeless. He helped the prostitutes. He fed the hungry." I hear them explaining to me, as Latoya did: "Millennials and Gen Z: We want to pray and act. I've seen generations of prayer and that's it. What are we going to do to ignite that prayer?" You and I have heard them crying out, as Liam did, "Forgive my French, but we are fucking scared, and we're fucking scared all the time. And institutions, whether they be religious, state or worldwide, they would do well to understand that, and to work directly with us, as opposed to just write off a Gen Z concern as us overreacting."

I also hear Archbishop William Temple asserting, "The church is the only society on earth that exists for the benefit of nonmembers." And I hear Jesus saying, "For those who want to save their life will lose it, and those who lose their life for my sake will find it" (Mark 8:35). Each of these voices is calling the church to take risks and make sometimes costly public claims about what is right and what is wrong, and to trust God will help us to reckon with the consequences and costs. What institutions are we maintaining with our silence and complicity? What relationships—with Nones and Dones, and with God—have we lost?

Some people will tell you the mainline, social justice-oriented Christian churches have suffered over the last thirty-five years because we got too vocal about politics. I don't think that's true, and the stats don't agree, either. If there was a political link, it's more likely that the Religious Right controlled the narrative about all things Christian, and the justice warriors didn't unequivocally ground our social stands on the person and witness of Jesus. The answer now is not to shift toward being more meek and apolitical, nor is it to become more partisan. Our only hope is to get more rooted in Jesus and then follow where he leads.

A word of warning: Following Jesus in the current political climate may very well lead you beyond the "purple." By purple, I mean the mixture of Democrats (blue) and Republicans (red) that exists in most mainline institutions. Alas, as of 2025, one of those respected, historic political parties has been overtaken by Christo-nationalism. There is no arguing this fact. That party's leaders regularly affirm the antithesis of the gospel of Jesus Christ, aggressively endorsing greed, vengeance, and lies and sacrificing the poor and most vulnerable on the altar of mammon and power. Anyone who stands for the truth of the gospel needs to reckon with that political reality.

People who say "keep politics out of the pulpit" don't understand that this is the ground on which we must now minister and lead in Jesus's name. As a result, there's no easy solution to the question of how to stay above politics, keep the pews happy, and speak the gospel truth. I return to what we've learned from Bishops Curry and Budde: stay close to Jesus and the Gospels, never engage in gratuitous name-calling and point-scoring, but when you have the opportunity to speak and make God's love known—even in a context that appears partisan—take a risk and speak. Silence and avoidance are no longer a viable Christian option.

Back It Up with Jesus-Shaped Life

All that said, the Nones and Dones I met want to see if we will do more than talk about God, justice, and love. They're encouraging us to live like Jesus and follow his way.

That call hasn't fundamentally changed since the first disciples heard Jesus's invitation to "come and see" (John 1:39). In The Episcopal Church, we flesh out those essentials in the Baptismal Covenant, a comprehensive set of promises that shape the life of every baptized person.[4]

- *Will you continue in the apostles' teaching and fellowship, in the breaking of bread, and in the prayers?* In other words, will you keep reflecting on scripture and allow God's word to shape your daily life? Will you keep praying and gathering for meals, and loving one another, even when it's hard? With God's help, we say, we will.
- *Will you persevere in resisting evil, and, whenever you fall into sin, repent and return to the Lord?* In other words, will you take seriously the idea that there are spiritual and worldly forces arrayed to lure us out of relationship with God? Will you resist their pull, say no to the call of greed, selfishness, and despair, and yes to the fullness of life with Jesus? With fear and trembling, and with God's help, we will.
- *Will you proclaim by word and example the Good News of God in Christ?* Especially today, the covenant is asking: Will you counter hate speech when it rolls off the tongues of your leaders or your friends? Will you fashion your life and words to point clearly to the love of God for *all*? It won't be easy, but with God's help, we will.
- *Will you seek and serve Christ in all persons, loving your neighbor as yourself?* Anyone can post a sign saying "All are welcome." Will you look for the face of Jesus in each person, including the one with whom you disagree? Will you also

see Jesus in the one who is transgender, Haitian, Indigenous, or in any way marginal? When someone tries to push the strangers out or to tell you they're the enemy, will you love and protect and serve them even more fiercely? With God's help, we will.

- And the final promise: *Will you strive for justice and peace among all people, and respect the dignity of every human being?* I love that our covenant is explicit and unapologetic about justice. God's justice was not invented by a political party; God's justice predates all that we humans could conjure. God's justice is for all people and all times, with particular heartbroken concern for widows, orphans, refugees, prisoners, the poor, the oppressed, and children. It does not seek to hoard and even increase the wealth of the rich rather than feed the poor. With God's help, we will stand with and for the most vulnerable in our midst.

Our first and most important response to the prophecy of the Nones and Dones is a radical return to promises like this and more broadly to the Way of Jesus. When we center on Jesus and rise from this foundation, we can more easily reorganize institutional priorities to put Jesus first, love God with our whole heart, protect the most vulnerable, and enter into solidarity with those being crucified in our day. When we prioritize becoming Jesus-shaped people gathered in Jesus-shaped communities following in a Jesus-led movement, no one will have to wonder where the Christians are. They'll know us by God's powerful, healing, self-giving, world-changing love working in us.

Our Institutions Can Innovate and Liberate

(Response to the Second Prophecy)

Institutions are not in and of themselves bad. I've seen them provide the infrastructure for lasting commitments to faith, justice, healing, and gospel love. Where would we be if the rag-tag group who followed Jesus hadn't formed churches, called leaders, shared resources, and grown to a worldwide movement capable of feeding, teaching, protecting, advocating, and honoring the image of God in people of every race and kind?

Even as we receive the Second Prophecy—"Stop Making Idols of Your Institutions, Buildings, Rules, and Dogma"—I don't hear these Nones and Dones rooting for the end of all institutions and structures. Remember the frustration Alex in Atlanta shared when she spoke of the anti-institutional movement popular among her young peers? She expressed gratitude that institutions "can do things at scale that individuals or small communities cannot. . . . [W]e don't have time to remake the world." She then countered the reign of expressive individualism with one sentence: "Frankly, saying my own life and experience is the only authority I can trust is exhausting." She may be surrounded on all sides by the Millennial zeitgeist, but she craves something more solid, rooted, and lasting than what she could create on her own.

So let us begin by saying institutions and sources of authority broader than the individual will have a place in the future of faith. What we cannot continue to abide—what I would submit has endangered us from the start—is idolatry toward our institutions and their associated structures, labels, rules, and dogmas. Jesus took care to warn his disciples, "The Sabbath was made for humankind and not humankind for the Sabbath, so the Son of Man is lord even of the Sabbath" (Mark 2:27–28). There have always been powers who wanted to control God's people by forcing them to bow to an incontrovertible rule, belief, structure, or leader. Jesus frees us from that tyranny.

Let's also be honest and admit that every church needs to be freed, because we all get rigid and even idolatrous about something. Evangelicals tend to be flexible and contextual around worship styles but shift into lockdown on doctrine and behavior. Mainline Protestants—especially my Episcopal family—would flip that script: We allow room for interpretation and contextuality regarding belief and behavior, but woe to those who step out of line around worship, structure, and/or policy. Roman Catholics have become increasingly rigid around both worship style (note the growing popularity of the Traditional Latin Mass) and belief and behavior (note the blowback against Pope Francis's perceived support for women and LGBTQ people).

Whatever your tradition, it's time to investigate where you're stuck and realize it's not just a matter of preference or culture. Our clinging to outdated and often self-serving structures and regulations has too often veered into idolatry. It endangers souls and limits our capacity to serve the cause of Jesus, which is to love God and love our neighbors as ourselves (Matthew 22). Every structure we build and every rule we craft should be assessed for alignment with this great commandment. Whatever we have built that does not contribute to that love, we need to reexamine, reimagine, and possibly release.

Embrace Fresh Approaches to Institutional Structure

In my experience serving The Episcopal Church, consulting for Lutherans, Congregationalists, and Presbyterians, and partnering with colleagues across an even broader ecumenical spectrum, the mountains of rules and policies governing our denominational bodies and congregations can smother the Spirit right out of a church. As Rev. Ryan Kuratko, the Episcopal chaplain at Columbia University, reminds us: "We set up all of these rules and canons for organizing our community life and for designating communities in certain ways as missions or parishes, etc. And a lot of those made great sense eighty years ago. They don't make as much sense now." What would serve faith in the future?

- Institutional bodies need to expand the definition of "church." English church leader Michael Moynagh posits a fuller vision for faith communities based on the biblical model of temples, synagogues, and tents. Blair Pogue and Dwight Zscheile explain how these different expressions can live in harmony in their book *Embracing the Mixed Ecology*:[1]

- *Temples* are "where people connect with the larger body of Christ–conferences, retreats, celebrations, pilgrimages, and websites. Just as Jesus went to the Jerusalem Temple periodically, so too believers engage these communal offerings and gatherings at times." I would also include cathedrals and large and/or well-resourced churches in this list. Sometimes we need to connect with a critical mass of people who share the faith and to experience more of Durkheim's collective effervescence in their midst.
- *Synagogues* in this model are "conventional local churches [with] a primary focus of spiritual connection and engagement." These traditional expressions will be vital to faith in the future, but they don't need to dominate the landscape as they do now. In too many churches, the pews are emptying, elders are tired, and resources are dwindling. We also hear younger generations saying they won't prop up church for the sake of church. As we will discuss in a moment, church leaders and members need to partner to proactively scale down the number of churches and buildings (as well as the number of dioceses and conferences) to more effectively respond to God's call in our rapidly changing contexts.
- *Tents* are "small worshiping communities within the spaces of daily life. Just as the people of Israel inhabited tents on the journey through wilderness, tents today may be fruitful for a period but also more flexible and adaptable than synagogues and temples." These tent ministries—picture

house churches and mission experiments—will be essential because they can more easily and fully partner with diverse neighbors and emerging, nonreligious communities. At a time when we're scaling down the number of traditional churches, we should increase the number of tents that dot the landscape and integrate them as essential components of a healthy body of Christ.

Each of these forms of church deserves respect and adequate support in the Christian ecosystem, because each will play a part in gathering, forming, and nourishing practicing Christian community in the future. Wherever possible, we should also make bold moves to redistribute resources, since temples/resourced institutions currently control the bulk of funds, synagogues/congregations hold just enough or struggle, and tents/contextual expressions tend to be impoverished. If we continue with that lopsided distribution, we are short-circuiting some of the best prospects for future mission.

- If you've got institutional power, use it to give your pioneers and innovators cover when they take risks for the gospel, rather than regulating, punishing, and forcing future-oriented leaders to hew to a narrow identity and role. Decision-makers should worry less about whether an action or proposal is adequately "Episcopal," "Presbyterian," or "Baptist." Ask more often whether and how it facilitates service to the gospel and to people who need God's love.
- Spread the word about rules that actually free people to minister across cultures, generations, and styles. The

Episcopal Church's General Convention passed a landmark resolution in 2015 allowing bishops to give congregations permission to use "Rite 3" for their main worship service.[2] The rite—known as "An Order for Celebrating the Holy Eucharist"—maintains the ancient liturgical essentials but allows significant local latitude for contextualization, including the use of a non-prayer book eucharistic prayer approved by the bishop. And yet, I've spoken to mission-focused bishops who bemoaned how the Prayer Book ties their hands on contextual worship. When I showed them the resolution, they were surprised and grateful. They had been telling people no when they could have said yes—yet more proof of how hard it is to reset a system that defaults to protect and guard itself and overregulate its leaders.

Embrace Fresh Approaches to Buildings

As anyone watching can see—and as those who know the church bottom line can attest—communities of faith spend a huge proportion of our time, heart, and money on our own houses of worship. It makes sense: Our buildings serve ministry, proclaim God's glory and majesty, and inspire the faithful and neighbors alike. What's also true: Aging church leaders are struggling to care for decrepit and expensive physical plants (if only the church could focus more on caring for these beloved elders!). As long as our priorities remain tilted toward building maintenance, we will have a hard time following the Lord who urged his disciples to travel lightly (Luke 10:4).

I can't begin to address the intricacies of church building management, consolidation, and closure here. What I can do is name some persistent realities and opportunities most every church will need to face sooner rather than later:

- *Do more with less.* How often have you seen multiple struggling churches of the same denomination nestled in close proximity? Sometimes it's a vestige from days when different cultures, classes, nationalities, and races couldn't or wouldn't worship together (let's face it: Those divisions aren't past tense). In other cases, we built for a population boom and now face a bust. Whatever the reasons, leaders must welcome congregations into brave truth-telling and healing to figure out how we got here, what has changed on the ground, and what sacrifices we can now make for the sake of God's future. Down the road, three churches partnering in one better-equipped building may prove to be more energizing and sustainable for members, and more winsome to the wider community.
- *Invest in the future.* When a building is sold, those who hold the purse strings are sorely tempted to pour all or even most of the proceeds into a general endowment. I pray and plead with you: Instead, consider directing a significant portion of those funds toward new ministry development, multicultural ministry, and/or vocations among emerging generations. In other words, invest in the underrepresented people and ministries we need for the future. If we're waiting for a rainy day to be more daring about deploying resources, look outside. Chances are very good that it's pouring where you are.
- *Partner up.* On-site community partnerships may be the key to new life and purpose for many of our buildings.

With help from experts like Trinity Church-Wall Street in New York,[3] congregations worldwide have found ways to embrace flexibility, host social enterprise, and sign real estate deals that allow the congregation to thrive alongside affordable housing, a day care facility, or a senior center. Yet another silver lining: Sharing space can open the door to deeper relationship with groups who otherwise wouldn't darken the church doorstep.

Negotiating closures, mergers, and ministry partnerships is a serious venture. Those who lead it well tend to be part hospice chaplain and part business tycoon. Still, we've got to find compassionate, just, and missional ways to reduce the number of buildings in our care and—in the process—to increase energy and resources for ministry.

Embrace Fresh Approaches to Leadership

Most mainline churches are suffering a dire clergy shortage. That deficit will only deepen as Baby Boomers continue to retire. Rather than focus primarily on recruiting more seminarians to attend three-year residential programs, learn languages no one on this continent speaks, and pass a multi-day written ordination certification exam, church leaders could take advantage of the crisis and leapfrog to opportunities like these:

- *Prepare the laity to serve as chaplains, evangelists, and ministry activators in their workplaces and ordinary lives.* That's Lindsey Hardegree's proposal in a thesis titled "Spirituality in Secular Spaces: Constructing a Practical Missional

Ecclesiology."[4] She asks, "Can the ministry of lay people bridge the gap between our increasingly declining church institutions and the robust spiritual expressions of people outside those institutions?" The answer should be a hearty yes!

Technically every ordained ministry leader is supposed to equip the laity for ministry and mission out in the world (Ephesians 4 urges people with specialized skills to use them to grow the ministry of *all* the saints). Alas, since clergy are so focused on institutional and internal life, and since the building itself is synonymous with "church," we tend to prepare lay leaders for ministry inside the church rather than outside in the world. From there, it's easy to see why outsiders and nonreligious people see us as self-absorbed and insular.

We can turn the tide not just by sending clergy out of the building more often but by equipping lay people to cultivate sacred awareness, make meaning, and organize ritual wherever they are. Hardegree is developing several tools for this equipping process, largely based on her work with a group of Marie Kondo consultants who discovered their client work feels like a ministry. We need more of these resources, and we need to prioritize getting them into the laity's hands. Lay people are the best-placed agents for advancing God's mission.

- *Build up a cadre of lay catechists.* Leaders across Africa, Asia, and Latin America have leaned into this order for decades, and it's one of the main reasons why their ministries expand exponentially. Lay catechists are trained, attached to a congregation, and provide discipleship formation, pastoral care, and community development in their local contexts. In some places, they have the flexibility to grow a new congregation that remains yoked to the main church. Ordained clergy still serve important roles, but this model allows for more extensive reach and requires far less institutional baggage.

- *Authorize ministers who are not in your "tribe."* Every day, another truly gifted leader is shunned by a conservative church because of their theology, ideology, or sexuality. Alas, when these leaders venture near an established church, instead of welcoming partnership and celebrating their gifts, denominations tend to toss out hoops and hurdles forcing them to bow, bend, and become exactly like us. That's a shame. Yes, we need accountability from anyone who would minister under the institution's umbrella. But we can also expand the umbrella's reach, embrace different formation models, and honor these leaders' track records as organizers and evangelists.

What could this look like? John Dorhauer of the United Church of Christ called his denomination to increase flexibility and responsiveness in their authorization and ordination process. As a result, they've been able to welcome leaders like Tricia Hersey, a Black Lives Matter activist who created the NAP ministry for front-line leaders in dire need of rest as resistance. Here's more good news: I recently attended a gathering of Black Lutherans and was shocked by how many participants came directly from established Pentecostal and evangelical ministries. In each case, the institution got more elastic around how it certified and formed leaders, which allowed them to more freely welcome ministries from emerging generations and nondominant cultures.

- Of course, we still need ordained leaders who rise from within a tradition. However, if they're going to minister effectively today, their formation should include theory and techniques for small group leadership, community building, social engagement and activism, asset-based community development, and even non-traditional skills like yoga certification, arts ministries, mental wellness chaplaincy, forest therapy, paperless music, dance, and more. And for everyone whose ministry would be enhanced by a summer working and reflecting in a traditional hospital Clinical Pastoral Education unit, there's someone else who would thrive in a community-based, organizing-informed CPE program. A few schools and judicatory bodies have experimented with this alternative track. More need to branch out and equip ministers to nurture faith in contemporary, post-Christian contexts.
- Leaders in every category and order—lay and ordained, rural and suburban, temple and tent—simply must be younger. In The Episcopal Church, the average newly ordained person is fifty.[5] If we know generational replacement isn't happening in our churches, why aren't institutions launching a dramatic, all-hands-on-deck push to honor and authorize young leaders for every ministry to which they might be called?

Shannon Kelly has rung this bell for much of her career in campus and young adult ministry. "They actually do want to be a part of institutions that speak to the things they care about," she said. "But church is not letting them

> lead, or it's making them jump through hoops. So they're out. Because of social media and our hyper-connected world, they have other ways of making connections and finding people to do the work they believe in. So we're missing out on a lot of innovation, passion, and energy because they're leaving." That's a loss for young people. It's a far greater loss for the church.

In the last chapter, Micah said the church needs to "change or die." My spin on this truth is that we need to change *and* die. Basically, Christians need to remember how to die to ourselves and the many attachments that draw us from the way of Jesus (and yes, some of those attachments are inside the church). We can take down the hurdles and stop grasping at idols. We can reimagine and refashion structures and institutions that innovate and liberate for the sake of the Jesus Movement. The future demands we take this leap of faith.

We Can Seek God Beyond the Walls

(Response to the Third Prophecy)

Because God became incarnate and dwelled among us in the flesh, we know that all of life—human, animal, plant, earth, waters, sky—is bathed in the glow of divine light. Any moment, any place, any person, could be the occasion for a God sighting. The Apostle Paul declared that truth with confidence when he wrote, "Ever since the creation of the world God's eternal power and divine nature, invisible though they are, have been seen and understood through the things God has made" (Romans 1:20).

So why do churches almost exclusively look for God inside our buildings and vessels? Why aren't we the first ones outside star-gazing and praising the heavens? Why aren't we the fiercest protectors of all the life-forms with whom we share God's world? Shouldn't we be walking around in wide-eyed awe at the miracle of humanity and speech and thought and everything God has done?

I hear that challenge in the Third Prophecy: "Go Meet the God Who Is Waiting Outside." Nones and Dones yearn for a lively engagement with the sacred in the natural world and in everyday life. How might our faith venture outside to join them . . . and God?

Voice Our Experiences of God in the Natural World

First, we need to get comfortable talking about how we've met God in nature and in the ordinary world. One of my favorite evangelism exercises is inviting people to tell a story of when they noticed the love or spirit of God. I keep expecting stories about a particular church hymn or the Eucharist or a prayer circle. Far more often, good old-fashioned church folk name a moment in nature (time with a loved one or in community is the only experience more spiritually evocative). So let's develop and share more earth-centered spirituality and provide people with more language and permission to claim those moments as holy and fully Christian.

Like a lot of religious professionals, I confess I initially filed these stories away under the category "people feel awe and wonder outside and call it God." But the power, specificity, and sheer holiness of their testimonies—including from people who have otherwise cut ties with religion—made me begin to wonder what God might be up to. God has been speaking to God's people in the wild beyond the bounds of formal religion all along. In fact, before there was religion, God communed with Adam and Eve in the Garden. Before there was Christianity, Mary met the risen Christ in the Garden. Why wouldn't people have experiences today like the ones our ancestors in faith describe?

Preachers can be the first to model this kind of testimony, and Jesus shows us how. His stories were saturated with images of the earth, animals, farming, cooking, and the whole of creation. You can picture the crowds nodding along as he spoke about the lilies of the field, the birds in the air, and the yeast in the bread—he was literally speaking about the everyday, natural things that make up their own lives.

We humans haven't changed much since then. Most people appreciate the way a full moon illuminates the darkness in the sky and maybe in our own lives. They know how a single flower springing up from concrete reminds us of resurrection. We know what it's like to be kids cooped up in the classroom for hours and then to finally be released to play outside at recess—that sounds a lot like heaven to me. If nonreligious and religious people collectively recognize these moments as genuinely sacred, preachers can come alongside and tether those experiences to the wider story of God and God's people throughout history.

But the faith of the future can't rely on authorized preachers to speak and listen for God's word in the world. I was inspired by Kimberley's earlier account of being "caught up in the spirit" while she was walking outside. Most of us have a version of that story, even if we wouldn't all use her terms. Who might be moved by your story? The only way to find out is for *all* of God's people to start telling the stories and warmly inviting neighbors to share theirs, too.

Prioritize Ministries That Get Us Outside

These ministries nourish our relationships with God. They're also the ideal third space (a social space that is not the home or work) for meeting nonreligious people and celebrating the spiritual vitality we humans experience in creation. When I asked colleagues and ministry leaders for suggestions, the list was so full, I could easily imagine spending week after week outside with God's people:

- *Camps and conference centers*: Individual churches and regional church bodies sponsor thousands of camps and conference centers across America. Many of them are endangered, which seems shortsighted considering that survey after survey tells us Americans experience the Spirit most powerfully in nature. Rev. Cody Maynus is the 35-year-old priest at All Saints Episcopal in Northfield, Minnesota, but he used to run a camp in the Diocese of South Dakota. He regularly witnessed young people with and without faith getting closer to God outside.

  > For the most part, people who came to us either as counselors or campers were not themselves religious. Their parents might have been, or they might have grown up in the church, but they largely weren't interested in religion. Certainly they weren't interested in doctrine or any of those things. But then we gathered in the chapel to sing, not the complicated songs, usually Taizé chants. The chapel looked out over this valley in the Black Hills. And there was such a palpable sense of the divine. Our kids, our counselors, they all got it.

  Rather than tucking camps and conference centers away on the margins of church life, we should be spotlighting them as critical sites for contemporary mission.

- *Outdoor worship*: You don't need to travel to the woods to worship and commune with God outdoors. During the pandemic, faith communities everywhere were forced to pack up and head outside for worship. Episcopal Church stats confirm that about 31 percent of churches still hosted an outdoor service at least once in 2023 (picture all those St. Francis Day social media posts).[1] It's a good habit to build, because outdoor services are a prime way to connect with nonreligious neighbors and to deepen our own witness to the glory, joy, freedom, and holiness we find in creation. There should be Eucharist in parks, on the church porch, and on the church lawn. If church kids and parents are at soccer games on Sundays, why can't we meet them for prayers and communion in the parking lot? Jesus gathered people for outdoor agape meals. We can surely host more holy picnics, blessing bread and wine and sharing with God's people in public.
- *Garden ministries*: Church gardens are often their most visible and celebrated offering to the community. And people's home gardens are often their most spiritually lively spaces. Why not bless that goodness? At the height of the COVID-19 pandemic, The Episcopal Church started "Good News Gardens," a movement for people who experience and share God's loving presence in relation to the land and its fruits. It was the perfect invitation when everyone was shut inside and starved for signs of life. My husband is a "Done," a former Roman Catholic who loves God and can't sit for an hour of worship to save his life. He pours his creativity and spiritual yearning into the small jungle now growing in our Harlem apartment. When he

heard me on a call talking about Good News Gardens, he perked up. When he saw the "GNG" garden posts we were sending around the country, he grabbed a set for his plants, drove them into the dirt, and proudly posted on social media that he was part of the Good News Gardens movement. How many other people are waiting for that invitation to join us and join God with our hands in the dirt?

- *Pet-friendly worship*: In her research on the spiritual lives of Nones, Elizabeth Drescher found that intimacy with pets is one of the most important ways nonreligious people connect with the holy. "Pets were generally viewed by Nones as compassionate, nonjudgmental companions to which their caregivers attributed remarkable degrees of intuition and empathy,"[2] Drescher noted. Given that close bond, it's worth exploring a wider variety of ways to welcome pets to worship.

  Every summer Sunday, St. John's Cathedral in Knoxville, Tennessee hosts "Dog Church," an outdoor worship gathering by the lakeshore that features bluegrass music and a warm welcome to dogs and their humans. "We wanted this to be an open service," said Rev. Thom Rasnick. "And by open, I mean not limited to any one particular denomination and really not limited to any one particular religion. There's a Christian feel to it, but it doesn't exclude anyone who might not be Christian."[3] The gathering is wildly popular among religious and nonreligious people alike, and it begs the question of what other partnerships churches and Nones could form to nurture spiritual and community life.

Commit to Addressing the Climate Crisis

Outdoor ministries are compelling, but they have to be yoked with justice and action. Young climate leaders literally carry the weight of the world on their shoulders, and they desperately seek partners—including traditional institutions—who are willing to address the crisis by their side.

Phoebe Chatfield is twenty-seven, a lifelong Episcopalian, and recently completed a term as The Episcopal Church's staff officer for creation justice. She shares her younger peers' impatience with religious institutions, particularly around eco-justice. "For young people, the ways the church is or is not working to stop climate change can impact their discernment about faith and staying involved," she said. "If the church is not meaningfully responding to the unraveling of ecosystems and a stable climate for future generations, what meaning can it offer to young people despairing about all of that?"

Phoebe is convinced that embracing the ministry of safeguarding the planet and vulnerable communities will lead toward new life. "There are so many opportunities here for the church to be revitalized through new forms of ministry and by following the lead of young people within and outside the church," she said. "Think of it: more intergenerational relationships, moral clarity, supporting local and global efforts, making space for climate grief. It's all part of building a peaceful world."

Celebrate the Sacred in Everyday Life

Everything I've described here about meeting and honoring God in the natural world also applies to meeting God in the mundane and everyday parts of our existence. Lots of people identify as spiritual but not religious not because they are disinterested in God but because they want a more expansive, all-encompassing spirituality than they could find within traditional religion. "The many SBNRs I met suggested they want a 're-sacralization' of the world," Linda Mercadante writes in *Belief without Borders: Inside the Minds of the Spiritual but not Religious*. "They want to see and experience the sacred in more areas of life. They want a spirituality which is vital."[4]

If we are looking for people comfortable sitting in church and talking about matters within those four walls, we shouldn't expect many young Nones and Dones to come flocking to our doors. But if we seek to nourish an incarnational spirituality deeply rooted in the earth and everyday life, Millennials and Gen Z seekers might be just ahead of us on the path, looking for companions.

Let's Dance

(Response to the Fourth Prophecy)

Remember Stephanie's clear proclamation to the churches: "You need to dance more"? The San Francisco-based None said she spent years witnessing Western Christianity's deep fear of the body and emotions, and it forced her to run the other way. By rendering the body suspicious and cutting us off from that source of power and wisdom, Christian leaders have also made the church dry and colorless. It's no coincidence that one of the only Christian groups growing in our time is the Pentecostal/Holiness movement, a more grassroots tradition born out of Los Angeles' Black community. That church knows how to dance—with each other and with the Holy Spirit.

Millennial and Gen Z Nones and Dones are urging the rest of America's churches to figuratively and literally dance together—in other words, to move, feel, touch, enjoy, weep, and above all, be authentic communities filled with the Spirit. That brings us to the Fourth Prophecy, "Form Loving, Embodied Communities That Welcome Our Whole, Authentic Selves."

How could we more fully welcome each other's authentic, diverse, embodied, passionate selves to belong and in the process welcome the vital presence of the Holy Spirit? The practical commitments that follow are a starting place. Feel free to also consult the Resource, Reflection, and Action Guide at www.stephaniespellers.com/church-tomorrow, which includes resources supporting groups who want to grow as authentic, embodied communities of love and belonging.

Prioritize the Formation of Authentic Communities of Love

We can begin by nurturing circles where people show up as their true, whole, embodied selves and celebrate that beauty and belovedness in others. The Nones and Dones I met are crying out for genuine communities of love, and I suspect the same longing thrums in the heart of most churchgoers. Have you ever seen a list of the things people appreciate about their church? The most popular words tend to be "community" and "love" and "welcome." When you ask about people's encounters with the sacred, as I did and as other researchers have with much larger samples, it often comes back to human relationships. We crave communities of love.

Jesus specialized in forming communities where people were deeply loved and deeply known. There was the Samaritan woman at the well, who spoke at length with Jesus and afterward ran to tell people, "Come and see a man who told me everything I have ever done!" (John 4:29). Jesus's fellow Jews never had the time of day for a woman like her, but he brought curiosity and humility to their exchange and treated her as a beloved child of God. He did the same for Zaccheus, a notorious tax collector shunned by his own people, hiding in a tree to catch a glimpse of Jesus. Jesus didn't see an enemy and sinner up there. He felt the lost man's yearning and said, "Zacchaeus, hurry and come down, for I must stay at your house today" (Luke 19:5). Zaccheus's life and the lives of his whole extended family changed because Jesus *saw* them, beheld them, listened to them. He loved them.

How much more do we need to be truly, authentically seen, beheld, heard, and loved in our day? Loneliness is officially an epidemic on par with the most serious public health crises. A remote life where I work at home, order groceries and meals to my door, engage in online social activities, read posts about others' lives, cancel plans with friends to stay in, pursue spiritual practices by myself—that may be a popular way to live, but it's not the way human beings thrive, and my conversation partners all knew it. The mystery was how to break the habit.

What if churches were known not *primarily* for our architecture or music, but as communities where people can reliably experience and practice radical love? It could happen if we prioritized love and invited people to descend Zacchaeus-like from their hiding places and isolation, take a risk, enter into community, know and be known by God and others. Some communities of love might own a building; others would not. Some might have no ordained leader, and even those with a pastor or priest would emphasize growing all of God's people as lovers of souls. Some might have fifteen in the circle, and others might have several thousand members, but both configurations would nourish intentional circles where people live a covenanted way of love together.

Churches can commit to several culture-shifting practices that form us into these kinds of communities. We can also set aside whatever prevents the growth of loving, authentic community in our midst.

- *Nurture participation and personal transformation*: The Millennial and Gen Z Nones and Dones I met don't have much patience with sitting, being preached at, or joining organizations that don't make an impact. They want to know how anything they adopt will improve their lives and heal the world, and they're not wrong to ask. Like scholar and pastor Linda Mercadante, I wonder if mainline American Protestant churches have set the bar too low, producing a wafer-thin spirituality that makes no demands and no impact. "If mainline churches are not attractive to [spiritual-but-not-religious people], perhaps such churches have adapted to our contemporary world all too well," Mercadante writes. "Trying so hard to be relevant, nondemanding, and friendly, they have downplayed the awe, respect, and humility we should feel in the presence of God."[1] Instead of pressing God into a small, convenient container that we open for an hour on Sundays, imagine if we welcomed the mysterious and powerful Holy Spirit to fill and shape our lives, our churches, and our world.
- *Form small groups*: Worship on Sunday morning cannot be the only moment to form or experience loving community (though there's plenty we can do to enhance the experience of loving community during worship—more on that in a moment). Small groups, cell groups, and house church gatherings are the ideal context within which to know

and be known, share our stories, commit to one another's flourishing, and increase accountability. These groups may form around a curriculum or class. They may share a common practice, interest, or ministry commitment. They may run from seven weeks to twenty years. They may meet in homes, at church, or online. This is where we share life and grow in love for God and one another.

- *Get rooted in our stories*: Stories are the soundtrack for any vital Christian community. If you look at places where people are forming community, making meaning and becoming fully known, you'll find stories. Preachers can model the power of story in the pulpit, including offering up our own personal, appropriate, self-revelatory stories. If the aim is not just to inform but to transform, and we know human minds and hearts are most profoundly affected by story, then I can't think why anyone would ever preach a sermon without connecting God's story in Scripture with the preacher's own story and the story of the community. Narratives like this are essential to cultivating a culture of sharing, vulnerability, trust, and love—in other words, a community.

  Story-sharing spaces and opportunities also need to extend beyond the pulpit. Try opening leadership meetings and small groups with one-to-one conversations where people share around meaningful questions. Take a moment in the middle of a sermon to invite people to turn to a partner and reflect on a story prompt that relates to the topic. Introduce story-sharing during your coffee hour—it would bring intentionality to the gathering and encourage people to break out of cliques. Everyone deserves the opportunity to discover how their story weaves together with God's story, and a true community is the group of people who want to hear that story from you.

- *Put the social back in social media*: Churches should be early adopters of technology and social media platforms, not to be cool but because we are committed to showing up wherever people are gathered. The caveat, as Rev. Zack Nyein of St. Bartholomew's Episcopal Church in New York advised, is to ensure the media facilitates social interaction. Social media was a powerful tool back when he and a group of students launched a campus ministry at the University of Tennessee in Chattanooga. "It allowed us to connect with each other, share with one another, figure out how we'd gather in real life." He said today's social media platforms highlight mostly one-way communication from an influencer to a group, generally with the goal of encouraging consumption. "Somewhere along the way, it became anti-social media." He hopes churches can be part of once again placing people and communities at the heart of social media.

Encourage Authentic, Embodied, Spirit-Filled Worship

As Jax in New York noted, worship should feel like authentic community, but in too many churches, it doesn't. Plenty of mainline Protestant churches preach the virtue of diversity, collaboration, and community, while the actual worship celebrates a single culture, lifts one or two primary (almost always professional) voices, and directs the group to listen to and value the one instead of the many. Then church leaders wonder why members who are gifted and powerful in other spheres sit in the pews waiting passively for religious professionals to make church happen. Why are we surprised that a clergy-centric liturgy forms a clergy-centric church? How could worship cultivate an authentic, participatory, trusting community of love?

- *All of the above:* So much of what we've already discussed about transformative community has special application to worship. Storytelling, worshipping outdoors, bringing pets to church, lay preaching, dancing, making art together, welcoming a wider range of cultural expressions—there are myriad ways to craft worship that welcomes people to bring their whole body, mind, and spirit before the God of life and love.
- *Gear to the children:* Early in my training for priesthood, I read a book called *Children at Worship: Congregations in Bloom.*[2] Everything Caroline Fairless recommended to make worship compelling with young people would also enliven the whole congregation. Speaking with Minneapolis school chaplain Rev. Katie Ernst convinced me once again that church worship in the future should look more like what ministers with young people—especially young, nonreligious people—are doing today. In every gathering, Ernst said she finds ways to engage our embodied wisdom, incorporates images and visuals, forms community through lightly accompanied group singing, decodes churchy language, and offers an authentic, specific welcome that includes people who are used to being excluded. You're never too young or too old for a worship community like that.

- *Worship in conjunction with community activities*: One way to shift your approach to worship is to take it out of the sanctuary and/or the Sunday slot. You can enhance participation and root worship in the life of the community by worshiping during community activities like Agape Meals or Holy Hikes.
- *Acknowledge that church is scary*: At every worship gathering, you should expect newcomers who have never been to church or spent time with Christians, and traumatized people who've been hurt by church but somehow made it to your sanctuary. Try to reexamine church through their eyes—or better yet, gently seek their feedback—and ensure the experience is as accessible and loving as possible.

  We needn't remove all that is beautiful, awesome, and mysterious in liturgical life, but we can prioritize the practice of holy hospitality to the stranger. A great way to begin eliminating barriers to welcome is with a hospitality audit—I've featured one in the online Resource, Reflection, and Action Guide.[3] And if these steps seem like too much extra work, just ask yourself, "What would an authentic community of love do?" And remember that what you do for the newcomer and irregular member will inevitably make worship more energizing and connective for regulars, too.

When did the audacious, revolutionary act of eating our Lord's flesh and drinking his blood turn into a rote activity? Why do we try to pass off deadening worship as "contemplative"? (As one friend observed: "Not every boring service is contemplative. Sometimes it's just boring.") What do we gain from our efforts to domesticate the Holy Spirit? As Susan Hope asserts, our communities can and should be "branded with, burned with, the conviction that Jesus is alive. This conviction may be held deeply and quietly, or it may bubble joyfully and exuberantly on the surface—but it must be there." Whether the dance is happening in the quiet of our hearts or out in the open, today we need to dance our way back into vibrant, Spirit-filled relationship with God and one another.

Before we leave this fourth and final prophetic call, there's a pressing question the Nones and Dones forced me to ponder, and you might've considered it by now, too. Most everyone wants to belong to an authentic community where they can be their real, whole selves. Alas, in the Age of Authenticity, nobody wants to commit. ***How do we form or grow communities of love in a culture that shuns membership, attendance, and commitment?***

I appreciate Linda Mercadante's guidance on this front: She recommends churches should help people to slowly shift "from shoppers to participants."[4] Shoppers drop in to pick up what they want and then head to whichever vendor satisfies the next craving. Participants literally take part. When churches focus on how well they provide services to members and guests—the best music by the most accomplished choir, the most beautiful building, the smartest preaching—they may be feeding the shopping impulse. If we prioritize community, stories, authentic presence, testimony, and transformation, and guests see a variety of people participating in ways that look like what they themselves could do, and regularly hear stories of changed lives, the shift can help to break the consumption cycle. The church isn't asking you to give or to help "them"; we are *all* the church, and the church only exists because we're in it together.

Mercadante goes on to predict that "membership itself may have to be rethought, perhaps changed to something like what the Shakers practiced, with concentric circles of participation from the 'gathering' order all the way to the fully committed. House churches, cell groups, and other creative alternatives to traditional structures may open up the reality of religious community to more people."[5] I believe she is inviting us to expand the definition of who is inside and who is outside. It's already happening, whether churches welcome the shift or not. Prior to the pandemic, a regular member might have attended once a month. Now they might come once a quarter. People who attend once a year may still consider themselves "members," even if the church administrator wonders if we should keep counting them in the parish report.

If the concentric circles are already emerging, can we be deliberate and expansive in our approach to these different modes of belonging? Some pioneers like Grace Cathedral in San Francisco are trying, and I've gathered and shared an array of best practices and hopeful experiments in the online Resource, Reflection, and Action Guide.

I am inspired and grateful for all the creative efforts to address a culture that no longer values commitment and embodied presence as part of belonging. We are also due for some honest reckoning. There is no true replacement for accountability and commitment in relationship, including our relationship with God. When we exercise the freedom to move constantly, chart our own paths, and hold loosely to commitments and people, we lose something along the way. Steadfastness—the spiritual virtue of sticking to what you've chosen or perhaps what has chosen you—may sound old-fashioned, but we surrender it at our peril. Commitment grows something unique, deep, and rich in our souls.

The culture of consumption doesn't want us to commit or be content with who we are or what we have. It needs us forever seeking what's next and what's better. The same restlessness causes us to reject any experience or community the moment we feel discomfort. Something better and less demanding is just around the corner, so walk away and pursue it. After a few months working with counselors at her diocesan camp in southern Ohio, my colleague Jerusalem Greer found she had to introduce a training unit on resilience. "They're not used to staying with something that's hard or makes them feel awkward. So when things get hard, they want to be up and out of here. I'm teaching them, 'You can do difficult things. Stay and find out.'"

Commitment isn't sexy or culturally *en vogue*, but it unlocks the door to a more mature, beautiful, meaningful, contented life. And community only works if each of us commits to showing up for one another. Faithful leaders need to have courage and issue an honest, personal, compelling invitation to loving, committed relationship with God in communities of love.

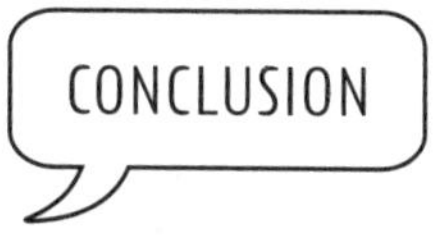

And You Shall Live

I began and titled this book with a question: *Church Tomorrow?* Now that we've reached the conclusion, I imagine you want some definitive answers. Will churches in the future be smaller sailing crafts, like dinghies capable of quickly adapting to their environment and darting in and out of tricky spaces? Will the only churches left be large, endowed luxury ships with the resources to withstand choppy waters, the ones that have enough financial security to take more risks without fear of losing Mrs. Grand-Dame's support?

And what of the Nones and Dones? Will the nonreligious emerging generations leapfrog traditional churches and create something else entirely, a different vehicle for faith and community care that today's church folk barely understand and really can't control? Will they make a hard right turn to churches that look creative and progressive and only later reveal their conservative ideology? Or will they turn to churches with smells, bells, and all things ancient, fascinated by a phenomenon that for them is fresh and fascinating?

Yes. And no.

The truth is, neither I nor a panel of experts can predict what a few hundred million Americans—including at least a hundred million nonreligious people—will do. Fifty years ago, numerous scholars might have warned you America was headed off the same secularized cliff as Europe. They were wrong. So while there will surely be fewer American Christians a generation from now, and certainly fewer members of the traditional mainline Protestant and evangelical churches, and likely some denominations will shrink to the point where they are hard to statistically track, I wouldn't dare to present a definitive sketch of *the* ideal church for the future.

Here is what I do know:

As I write these concluding words, it has been five years almost to the day since I began my last book, *The Church Cracked Open*. At that time—summer 2020—we were deep in the heart of the COVID-19 pandemic, and I honestly hoped the combination of a global health tragedy, historic racial reckoning, and systemic institutional decline might together crack the church-as-we've-known-it into enough pieces that we could partner with God to shape a different, Jesus-centered church. Five years later, much has changed but more has not. A racialized backlash is hell-bent on overturning the gains of every twentieth-century movement for freedom and compassion. Meanwhile, churches are hustling to reclaim pre-pandemic ways of life and tinkering in the face of systemic loss.

Today, I have a deeper respect for institutional willingness to resist the very transformation that will save our lives. *And* I am absolutely convinced that God is not finished with God's church, including the American Protestant mainline. If anything, though the valley of dry bones spreads all around, we may be closer to God's future now than ever before. In times like these, I find myself listening to praise songs about the resurrection power of God. I trust the God who rolled away the stone and made life flourish at the grave. The God who led the Israelites through the Red Sea on dry land. The God who breathed into a valley of dry bones and declared, "You shall live!" It would seem that our endings are God's beginning.

God knows, it hurts to witness mass disaffiliation from civic and religious organizations that once stood as signs of American enlightenment, virtue, and progress. And yet, the more we recognize the limits of our own programs, power, and proficiency, the more we can admit how much we need God, which is the beginning of true wisdom and new life. Wasn't that one of Jesus's primary teachings? He promised in the Beatitudes that those who admit their poverty will receive the very kingdom of heaven (Matthew 5:3). When Pharisees criticized him for dining with tax collectors and sinners, he taught that the physician comes to heal those who recognize their sickness (Mark 2:17, Luke 5:31, Matthew 9:12). In our weakness, God's power shines.

At the very same time, perhaps after we reach the limit of our internal capacity, we might finally take seriously the many people outside of church, listen to their stories, attend to their wisdom and struggle, and admit how much we need one another. When the pews are more empty than full, church folk might be willing to question the sacred cows, let go of something that needed to die, and embrace that which is life-giving and holy to the generations and cultures just beyond our walls. When we are no longer dominant, we might at last be needy and humble enough to acknowledge The Other's gifts, power, and presence. Only then is mutuality possible. Only then can we all join in co-creating tomorrow's church.

The good news I hope you hear now is, those "others" just beyond the church are often eager to speak with us. I came to dozens of Millennial and Gen Z Nones and Dones as a stranger with four provocative yet simple questions, and one after another, they poured out their hearts. I invited them to share a word with the church, and they didn't just peace-out with a one-star Yelp review. They collectively offered guidance that could lead us to become more powerful and faithful communities of love with a credible witness in a hurting world. It makes me wonder what you might learn if you spoke to the young (and not-so-young) Nones and Dones in your orbit. What partnerships might be born? How might God add a blessing at the very moment you thought all was lost, through the one you deemed lost?

Someone out there will offer you guarantees, crystal balls, and a ten-point plan for success. Don't believe the hype. Here, I offer the fervent prayer that you will go forth with curiosity and love. Go and be uncertain and vulnerable, and let the stranger host you. Go and ask questions you don't know the answer to, with people whose wisdom you long ignored. Go and discover new elements of your own story, revealed in the fertile space between you and The Other.

Please, my friends, go to reclaim and proclaim a faith rooted in the life and love of Jesus. Go be real, embodied, and full of delight in the Spirit and in one another. Go free of the need to maintain what God never asked you to maintain. Go sit by the riverbank and sing your song. Go and discover God was there all along.

Acknowledgments

At each stage in the research and writing of *Church Tomorrow?*, a community gathered around to offer precisely the wisdom, connections, feedback, encouragement, and hospitality I needed in order to keep going. I love you all and am grateful to celebrate here what we have done together.

Thanks to my Church Publishing family, particularly publisher Airié Stuart and executive editor Fiona Hallowell. You welcomed this project, pushed me to dream bigger, asked the right questions, believed in my witness, and served as professional and spiritual companions.

Thanks to the Executive Leadership Team of The Episcopal Church. This project was born late in the summer of 2024, as I was transitioning out of service alongside then-Presiding Bishop Michael Curry and as Presiding Bishop-elect Sean Rowe was coming on board. The entire Executive Leadership Team, especially the Reverend Canon Michael Barlowe, who was wrapping his time as Executive Officer of the General Convention, saw the potential in this project and advocated for me to receive a writing leave in my final three months on staff. If any of you had said no, this book would not be here today. Your faith gave me faith.

I originally applied for a Louisville Institute pastoral project grant to support my research and writing. Dwight Zscheile and Courtney Cowart cheered me on, helped to refine the proposal and wrote recommendation letters for my application. I did not receive the grant, but their scholarship and leadership—starting with the application process and flowing into the actual writing journey—was a guiding light, and their friendship means the world to me.

Huge thanks to all the "connectors" who linked me with Nones and Dones across the country. If you see (!), that's someone who helped me to link with multiple conversation partners:

- *Atlanta host*: Courtney Cowart. *Atlanta connectors:* Courtney Cowart, Ann Cramer (!), Monique Moultrie, Zack Nyein, Sunday Assembly-Atlanta leadership (especially Ross Llewallyn!), Holle Tubbs, Winnie Varghese.
- *Twin Cities host*: Jenn Olson. *Twin Cities connectors:* Andy Barnett, Lydia Bucklin, Tony Jones, Craig Loya, Cody Maynus (!) and All Saints Episcopal Church in Northfield, Blair Pogue, Jennifer Olson, Chris Sikkema, Dwight Zscheile.
- *New York hosts*: Albert deGrasse and our feline overlords Miles Davis and Pauli Murray. *New York connectors:* Shana Kaplanov, Shannon Kelly, Ryan Kuratko, Sophia Longmuir, Jeannine Otis, St. Bartholomew's Episcopal Church, Teagan Sage.
- *San Francisco hosts*: Austin and Maleah Rios. *San Francisco Bay Area connectors:* Miguel Bustos, Amy Cook, Kevin Deal, Elizabeth Drescher (!), Eric Metoyer, Cameron Partridge, Eva Slavitt (!), Travis Stevens (!), Malcolm Young.
- *Other connectors*: Joyce Cheng (!), Nick Gordon.

May God add an extra portion of blessing for the Spirit Circle! Since year one of the pandemic, I've been privileged to meet every other week with a small group that includes Jimmy Bartz, Don Edwards, Lisa Kimball, Aaron Niequist, and Sophfronia Scott. We gather to pray and reflect on Scripture and our vocations, which means they were among the first to hear of this project. Their prayers brought it to life.

And thanks be to God for the Spirit and Data Team! Jerusalem Greer, Zack Nyein, and Katie Nakamura Rengers joined me at Trinity Retreat Center to comb through data and narratives. Friends: You read your assignments, helped me to make sense of the mountain of interview transcripts and notes from books and articles, assisted with crafting the detailed book outline, and generally made this labor a true joy.

I kiss the ground and give thanks for each of the locations and communities where this book was truly birthed and written:

- *St. Columba's Episcopal Church in Inverness, California* received me at their gorgeous, contemplative retreat house in January 2025 when I needed a quiet place to complete my literature review (in other words, to read and notate an average of two books a day for eight days). Vicar Vincent Pizzuto and administrator extraordinaire Anna Haight welcomed me with prayer, food, shelter, wine, and laughter, and set me on the course that led to this day.
- *Trinity Wall Street Retreat Center in Cornwall, Connecticut* offered its signature, gracious hospitality to me and the circle of readers who gathered in February to review data and narratives. I am forever grateful for the kindness and

generosity of Trinity clergy and friends Michael Bird and Mark Bozzuti-Jones.

- *The Folly in Greenville, Mississippi.* Courtney Cowart handed me the keys to her writing cottage in the Mississippi Delta and provided the space and stillness I needed to write the first two-thirds of the book in March. It must be noted that The Folly (yes, this cottage has a name and a story) belonged to Courtney's beloved friend Julia Reed, a writer for *Vogue* and *Newsweek*, author of numerous books, teller of great tales, and one of the great Southern hostesses of her generation. Courtney promised something in that brown Delta water makes for good writing. I pray I did Julia proud.
- *The Secrets Resorts in Playa del Carmen and Playa Mujeres.* I joined this vacation club many, many moons ago, and they're now used to me sitting alone with a laptop at dinner. ¡Bendiciones, mis amigos!
- *Harlem* is my home here in New York. I thought I needed to get away to write well, but then I remembered the many Black artists who created magic during the Harlem Renaissance. I am grateful to stand on their shoulders.

Props, kudos, and great love to my cheerleaders, editors, and co-conspirators. Dear friends and family, you received rounds of drafts and were honest about what landed and what needed work, and kept insisting that the church needs this book. Thank you Paige Blair-Hubert (!), Mark Bozzuti-Jones, Eva Cavaleri, Arrington Chambliss, Courtney Cowart (!), Lynn Campbell, Catherine Clay, Mary Clay, Julie Cudahy-Longmuir, Albert deGrasse, Julie Hoplamazian, Jane Gould (!), Jerusalem Greer,

Bradley Mattson, Katie Nakamura Rengers, Zack Nyein, Tamara Plummer (!), Blair Pogue (!), Calvin Sanborn, Daniel Summers, Dwight Zscheile (!).

I can't offer enough gratitude and respect to Kristin LeMay, who designed the beautiful charts and graphics, offered piercing editorial insight, and practically skipped with me across the finish line. Maybe someday we'll write a book together. Wait—I think we just did.

And finally, always and forever, I give thanks for my husband and partner, Albert. You were patient and curious when I sat at the beach reading philosophical tomes. You provided professional-grade shoulder rubs when I took over the sofa and really the entire living space of our Harlem apartment for weeks at a time. Above all, you were the generous, protective partner who insisted I take this time, whether to conduct a project, write a book, or just breathe. I'm lousy at stopping and receiving, but you keep teaching me and cracking me open with your love. I can't wait to return the favor when it's time for "Now Driving: The U.S.A." My Boo—you're so outrageous!

Endnotes

Introduction

1. "How Religious Are Americans?," Gallup, March 24, 2024, https://news.gallup.com/poll/358364/religious-americans.aspx.
2. "Decline of Christianity in the U.S. Has Slowed, May Have Leveled Off: Findings from the 2023–2024 Religious Landscape Study," Pew Research Center, February 26, 2025, https://www.pewresearch.org/religion/2025/02/26/decline-of-christianity-in-the-us-has-slowed-may-have-leveled-off.
3. Ryan Burge, "Religion in 2024: The Plateau Is Real," Graphs About Religion, April 7, 2025, https://www.graphsaboutreligion.com/p/religion-in-2024-the-plateau-is-real.
4. Ryan Burge, "Just How Bad Is Denominational Decline?," Graphs About Religion, June 12, 2023, https://www.graphsaboutreligion.com/p/just-how-bad-is-denominational-decline.
5. United Methodist Church Data, accessed September 8, 2025, https://www.umdata.org/charts?jur=all&start=2023&end=2023.

Chapter 1

1. Alexis de Tocqueville, *Democracy in America*, ed. J. P. Mayer, trans. George Lawrence (HarperCollins, 2000), 291.
2. Roger Finke and Rodney Stark, *The Churching of America, 1776–2005: Winners and Losers in Our Religious Economy* (Rutgers University Press, 2005), 29.

3. Several of the founders were what scholars now describe as "theistic rationalists," meaning they affirmed a powerful, rational, and benevolent Creator who engaged in human affairs, but they disavowed Christ's divinity, the Trinity, original sin, the atonement, and other central tenets of Christan faith. I appreciate Gregg Frazer's work on this topic, especially his book *The Religious Beliefs of America's Founders: Reason, Revelation, and Revolution* (University Press of Kansas, 2012).
4. De Tocqueville, *Democracy in America*, 295.
5. "Decennial Census Historical Facts," United States Census Bureau, https://www.census.gov/programs-surveys/decennial-census/decade/decennial-facts.2020.html#list-tab-1813000050, as cited in Jim Davis et al., *The Great Unchurching: Who's Leaving, Why Are They Going, and What Will It Take to Bring Them Back?* (Zondervan, 2023), 4.
6. Finke and Stark, *The Churching of America*, Figure 1.2, 23.
7. *Encarta 2000 New World Almanac*, as cited in Robert Putnam, *Bowling Alone: Revised and Updated: The Collapse and Revival of American Community* (Simon & Schuster, 2001), 385.
8. Putnam, *Bowling Alone*, 18.
9. Putnam, *Bowling Alone*, 268.
10. Robert Ellwood, *The Fifties Spiritual Marketplace: American Religion in a Decade of Conflict* (Rutgers University Press, 1997), as cited in Carol Tucker, "The 1950s—Powerful Years for Religion," *USC Today*, June 16, 1997, https://today.usc.edu/the-1950s-powerful-years-for-religion.
11. Stephen Koeth, "Postwar Building Boom," *Sacred Architecture Journal* 34 (Fall 2018), https://www.sacredarchitecture.org/articles/postwar_building_boom.
12. "How Religious Are Americans?"
13. Wade Clark Roof and William McKinney, *American Mainline Religion: Its Changing Shape and Future* (Rutgers University Press, 1987), 12.
14. "How Religious Are Americans?"
15. "Decline of Christianity in the U.S. Has Slowed."
16. "How Religious Are Americans?"
17. "Decline of Christianity in the U.S. Has Slowed."

18. Burge, "Just How Bad Is Denominational Decline?"
19. Burge, "Just How Bad Is Denominational Decline?"
20. "Decline of Christianity in the U.S. Has Slowed"
21. Burge, "Religion in 2024: The Plateau Is Real."
22. As of 2025, some researchers and news outlets are reporting signs of young people returning to church, especially young men. See Ruth Graham, "In a First Among Christians, Young Men Are More Religious Than Young Women," *The New York Times*, September 25, 2024, https://www.nytimes.com/2024/09/23/us/young-men-religion-gen-z.html; Catherine Pepinster, "'The Quiet Revival,'" Religion Media Centre (UK), April 8, 2025, https://religionmediacentre.org.uk/news/the-quiet-revival-huge-increase-in-young-people-attending-church. Note that most gains are among Roman Catholics and Pentecostals, not mainline Protestants or traditional evangelicals.
23. Burge, "Religion in 2024: The Plateau Is Real."
24. Over a seventeen-year period—from 2007 to 2024—the Pew Research Center has noted a pattern of Americans becoming less religious as they age, not more religious. See the graphic at https://www.pewresearch.org/religion/2025/02/26/decline-of-christianity-in-the-us-has-slowed-may-have-leveled-off.
    - People born in the 1940s were ages 58–67 when they were polled in 2007. At that point, they reported high rates of daily prayer (65 percent) and Christian affiliation (86 percent) and fairly few Nones (10 percent). By 2024, they prayed less often (58 percent pray daily) and were less likely to identify as Christian (80 percent), and the Nones in their midst grew to 13 percent.
    - The same trendline repeats for every age group, only with successively lower starting points for daily prayer and Christian identification, and higher starting points for being nonreligious.
    - Americans born in the 1990s were age 18–24 when they spoke to the Pew Center in 2014. At the time, 39 percent said they prayed daily, 56 percent said they were Christian and 36 percent were already identifying as Nones. In the 2023–24 study, the same group was less likely to pray daily (31 percent) and had nearly an equal likelihood of being Christian (46 percent) or a None (44 percent).

The most recent cohort was born in the 2000s and was age 18–24 when they were surveyed in 2024. They entered the picture with the lowest rate of daily prayer (27 percent) and aligned with their next youngest counterparts on religious identity (46 percent Christian; 43 percent None). While we don't have multiple survey results for this cohort (that'll come in seven to ten years), if you compare them with 18- to 24-year-olds surveyed just ten years earlier, there is a shocking ten-point drop in Christian affiliation and a seven-point bump in the percent who said they have no religion.

25. "Religious Switching," subhead in "Decline of Christianity in the U.S. Has Slowed, May Have Leveled Off," Pew Research Center, February 26, 2025, https://www.pewresearch.org/religion/2025/02/26/religious-switching.
26. Religious Landscape Study 2023–24, "Religious Composition by Race," Pew Research Center, https://www.pewresearch.org/religious-landscape-study/racial-and-ethnic-composition/.
27. Religious Landscape Study, 2023–24, "Religiously Unaffiliated Religious Nones," Pew Research Center, https://www.pewresearch.org/religious-landscape-study/religious-tradition/religiously-unaffiliated-religious-nones/.
28. Daniel A. Cox and Kelsey Eyre Hammond, "Young Women Are Leaving Church in Unprecedented Numbers," American Survey Center Newsletter, April 4, 2024, https://www.americansurveycenter.org/newsletter/young-women-are-leaving-church-in-unprecedented-numbers. For a more in-depth take on this topic, see Sarah McCammon's *The Exvangelicals: Loving, Living, and Leaving the Evangelical Church*.
29. "Party Identification Among Religious Groups and Religiously Unaffiliated Voters," subhead in "Changing Partisan Coalitions in a Politically Divided Nation," Pew Research Center, April 9, 2024, https://www.pewresearch.org/politics/2024/04/09/party-identification-among-religious-groups-and-religiously-unaffiliated-voters.
30. "Who Are the 'Nones' and How Are They Defined?" subhead in "Religious Nones in America: Who They Are and What They Believe," Pew Research Center, January 24, 2024, https://www.pew

research.org/religion/2024/01/24/who-are-the-nones-how-are-they-defined.

31. Ryan Burge, "Let's Have a Look at Education and Religious Attendance," Religion Unplugged, September 2023, https://religionunplugged.com/news/2023/9/12/education-lets-have-a-talk-about-religious-attendance.
32. "Religious Nones in America: Who They Are and What They Believe," Pew Research Center, January 24, 2024, https://www.pewresearch.org/religion/2024/01/24/religious-nones-in-america-who-they-are-and-what-they-believe.
33. "Religious Nones in America."
34. "Religious Nones in America."
35. "Religious and Spiritual Beliefs," subhead in "Decline of Christianity in the U.S. Has Slowed," Pew Research Center, February 26, 2025, https://www.pewresearch.org/religion/2025/02/26/religious-and-spiritual-beliefs/.

Chapter 2

1. Burge, "Religion in 2024: The Plateau Is Real."
2. "Decline of Christianity in the U.S. Has Slowed."
3. Daniel Cox, Jacqueline Clemence, and Eleanor O'Neil, "The Decline of Religion in American Family Life," American Enterprise Institute, December 11, 2019, https://www.aei.org/research-products/report/the-decline-of-religion-in-american-family-life/.
4. Ibid.
5. Charles Taylor, *A Secular Age* (Belknap Press, 2007), 471.
6. Ibid., 476.
7. Ibid., 299.
8. Ibid., 486.
9. Christian Smith, *Why Religion Went Obsolete: The Demise of Traditional Faith in America* (Oxford University Press, 2025), 2.
10. Ibid., 4.
11. Ibid., 148.
12. Ibid., 336.
13. Ibid., 337.

14. James Emery White, *The Rise of the Nones* (Baker Books, 2014), 48.
15. Tay Keong Tan, "Silence, Sacrifice and Shoo-Fly Pies: An Inquiry into the Social Capital and Organizational Strategies of the Amish Community in Lancaster County, Pennsylvania" (Ph.D. dissertation, Harvard University, 1998), as cited in Robert Putnam, *Bowling Alone: The Collapse and Revival of American Community: Revised and Updated* (Simon and Schuster, 2020), 233.
16. Putnam, *Bowling Alone*, 222.
17. "Dopamine," Cleveland Clinic, last reviewed March 23, 2022, https://my.clevelandclinic.org/health/articles/22581-dopamine.
18. Danielle Page, "What Happens to Your Brain When You Binge-Watch a TV Series," NBC News, November 4, 2017, https://www.nbcnews.com/better/health/what-happens-your-brain-when-you-binge-watch-tv-series-ncna816991.
19. Christian Smith, Millennial Zeitgeist Survey, results in *Why Religion Went Obsolete*, 139.
20. Brené Brown, *Braving the Wilderness: The Quest for True Belonging and the Courage to Stand Alone* (Random House, 2017), 54.
21. Vivek Murthy, "Our Epidemic of Loneliness and Isolation: U.S. Surgeon General's Advisory on the Healing Effects of Social Connection and Community," Office of the U.S. Surgeon General, 2023, 4, https://pubmed.ncbi.nlm.nih.gov/37792968/.
22. Derek Thompson, "The Antisocial Century," *The Atlantic Monthly*, February 2025, 4, https://www.theatlantic.com/magazine/archive/2025/02/american-loneliness-personality-politics/681091/.
23. Patrick Sharkey, "Homebound: The Long-Term Rise in Time Spent at Home Among U.S. Adults," January 2024, *Sociological Science* 11, 553–78, as cited in "The Antisocial Century," 15.
24. Peter Berger, *The Sacred Canopy: Elements of a Sociological Theory of Religion* (Open Road Media, 2011), originally published 1967, 107.
25. Ryan Burge, "The Religious Composition of the Political Parties Over the Last 50 Years," Graphs About Religion, based on analysis of the General Social Survey 1972–2018, November 6, 2023, https://www.graphsaboutreligion.com/p/the-religious-composition-of-the.
26. Michael Hout and Claude Fischer, "Explaining Why More Americans Have No Religious Preference: Political Backlash and Generational

Succession, 1987–2012," *Sociological Science* 1 (October 2014), https://www.sociologicalscience.com/download/volume%201/october/SocSci_v1_423to447.pdf.

27. Ibid.
28. Jay Demerath, "Cultural Victory and Organizational Defeat in the Paradoxical Decline of Liberal Protestantism," *Journal for the Scientific Study of Religion*, 34(4): 458–69, as cited in *Why Religion Went Obsolete*, 102.
29. "The Changing Demographic Composition of Voters and Party Coalitions," Pew Research Center, April 9, 2024, https://www.pewresearch.org/politics/2024/04/09/the-changing-demographic-composition-of-voters-and-party-coalitions/.
30. White, *The Rise of the Nones*, 50.

Part II

1. See the comprehensive, often multi-year research of Elizabeth Drescher, *Choosing Our Religion: The Spiritual Lives of America's Nones* (Oxford University Press, 2016); Linda Mercadante, *Belief without Borders: Inside the Minds of the Spiritual but Not Religious* (Oxford University Press, 2014); Christian Smith, *Why Religion Went Obsolete*; Sue Pizor Yoder and Co.lab.inc., *Hear Us Out: Six Questions on Belonging and Belief* (Fortress Press, 2023).
2. "Party Identification Among Religious Groups and Religiously Unaffiliated Voters," subhead in "Changing Partisan Coalitions in a Politically Divided Nation," Pew Research Center, April 9, 2024, https://www.pewresearch.org/politics/2024/04/09/party-identification-among-religious-groups-and-religiously-unaffiliated-voters/.
3. "Age, Generational Cohorts and Party Identification" subhead in "Changing Partisan Coalitions in a Politically Divided Nation," Pew Research Center, April 9, 2024, https://www.pewresearch.org/politics/2024/04/09/age-generational-cohorts-and-party-identification/.

Chapter 3

1. Tara Isabella Burton, *Strange Rites: New Religions for a Godless World* (PublicAffairs, 2020), 69.
2. Ibid., 32.

Chapter 4

1. Casper ter Kuile, *The Power of Ritual: Turning Everyday Activities into Soulful Practices* (HarperCollins, 2020), 28.
2. Springtide Research Institute, *State of Religion & Young People: Exploring the Sacred* (Springtide, 2023), 6.
3. Giselle Abramovich, "Redefining Health through Vitality: New Insight into Five Years of Loneliness Trends," The Cigna Group Newsroom, October 2023, https://newsroom.thecignagroup.com/vitality-research-new-insight-into-five-years-of-loneliness.
4. Springtide, *State of Religion*, 28.
5. Claire Gecewicz, "'New Age' Beliefs Common Among Both Religious and Nonreligious Americans," Pew Research Center, October 1, 2018, https://www.pewresearch.org/short-reads/2018/10/01/new-age-beliefs-common-among-both-religious-and-nonreligious-americans.
6. Jenny Odell, *How to Do Nothing: Resisting the Attention Economy* (Melville House, 2019).

Chapter 5

1. Emile Durkheim, *The Elements of Religious Life* trans. by Joseph W. Swain (Ruskin House, 1912), 245–51.
2. "Religious 'Nones' in America: Who They Are and What They Believe," Pew Research Center, January 24, 2024, https://www.pewresearch.org/religion/2024/01/24/religious-nones-in-america-who-they-are-and-what-they-believe.
3. Sunday Assembly Atlanta homepage, accessed September 8, 2025, https://www.sundayassemblyatlanta.org.

Part III

1. Global Mission Staff of the Evangelical Lutheran Church in America, "The Accompaniment Model of Mission," *Word & World* 25, no. 1 (Spring 2005), 203.
2. Learn more in: Stephanie Spellers, *Radical Welcome: Embracing God, The Other and the Spirit of Transformation—15th Anniversary Edition* (Church Publishing, 2021).

Chapter 6

1. Rebecca Revell, "Why Don't Young Adults Go to Church Anymore?," *Rebecca Said So* (blog), January 24, 2025, https://rsaidso.blogspot.com/2025/01/why-dont-young-adults-go-to-church.html.
2. Presiding Bishop's Office and Ipsos Research, "Jesus in America Survey," The Episcopal Church, 2022, https://www.episcopalchurch.org/home-3.

Chapter 7

1. Revell, "Young Adults."

Chapter 8

1. Meister Eckhart (1260–1328) in *Earth Prayers: 365 Prayers, Poems, and Invocations from Around the World*, eds. Elizabeth Roberts and Elias Amidon (HarperOne, 1991), 251.

Chapter 10

1. "The Jesus Movement," The Episcopal Church, October 20, 2021, www.episcopalchurch.org/jesus-movement.
2. Michael Curry, *Following the Way of Jesus: Church's Teachings for a Changing World*, volume 6 (Church Publishing, 2017), 8.
3. Inaugural Prayer Service, Washington National Cathedral, January 21, 2025. https://www.youtube.com/watch?v=xwwaEuDeqM8.
4. 1979 Book of Common Prayer (Church Publishing, 1979), 305.

Chapter 11

1. Dwight Zscheile and Blair Pogue, *Embracing the Mixed Ecology: Inherited and New Forms of Christian Community Flourishing Together* (Seabury Books, 2025), 67, drawing on Michael Moynagh, *Church for Every Context* (SCM Press, 2012), 85.
2. 79th General Convention of The Episcopal Church: 2015, Resolution D050, accessed on April 8, 2025, https://www.episcopalarchives.org/cgi-bin/acts/acts_resolution.pl?resolution=2015-D050.

3. Consult Trinity Church Wall Street's grants and programs to support churches that seek to repurpose buildings in alignment with bold mission, https://trinitychurchnyc.org/community/how-we-partner/mission-real-estate-development.
4. Lindsey Hardegree, *Spirituality in Secular Spaces: Constructing a Practical Missional Ecclesiology: D. Min. Dissertation* (Candler School of Theology, Spring 2024), 12, https://etd.library.emory.edu/concern/etds/kd17cv22k?locale=en.
5. Data provided directly by Office of the Recorder of Ordinations, Church Pension Group.

Chapter 12

1. "Analysis of the 2023 Parochial Report Data," The Episcopal Church, 2023, https://www.episcopalchurch.org/wp-content/uploads/2024/11/Analysis-of-the-2023-Parochial-Report-Data-final-draft.pdf.
2. Elizabeth Drescher, *Choosing Our Religion: The Spiritual Lives of America's Nones* (Oxford University Press, 2016), 139.
3. Rev. Thom Rasnick featured in video "Dog Church—Sundays by the Shore," accessed September 8, 2025, https://www.youtube.com/watch?v=r1UymHIy7wk. Learn more about Dog Church at https://dogchurchknox.com/.
4. Linda Mercadante, *Belief without Borders: Inside the Minds of the Spiritual but not Religious* (Oxford University Press, 2014), 251.

Chapter 13

1. Mercadante, *Belief without Borders*, 251.
2. Caroline Fairless, *Children at Worship: Congregations in Bloom* (Church Publishing, 2000).
3. See "Hospitality 101: Inviting, Greeting and Incorporating," The Episcopal Church Evangelism Office, accessed June 18, 2025, https://www.episcopalchurch.org/wp-content/uploads/2020/12/evangelism_hospitality_101_and_assessment.pdf.
4. Mercadante, *Belief without Borders*, 257.
5. Ibid, 257.

Bibliography

Books

Berger, Peter. *The Sacred Canopy: Elements of a Sociological Theory of Religion*. Open Road Media, 2011. Originally published 1967.

Brown, Brené. *Braving the Wilderness: The Quest for True Belonging and the Courage to Stand Alone*. Random House, 2017.

Bullivant, Stephen. *Nonverts: The Making of Ex-Christian America*. Oxford University Press, 2022.

Burge, Ryan. *The Nones: Where They Came From, Who They Are, and Where They Are Going*. Fortress Press, 2023.

Davis, Jim, Michael Graham, and Ryan Burge. *The Great Dechurching: Who's Leaving, Why Are They Going, and What Will It Take to Bring Them Back?* Zondervan, 2023.

Burton, Tara Isabella. *Strange Rites: New Religions for a Godless World*. PublicAffairs, 2020.

Curry, Michael. *Following the Way of Jesus*: *Church's Teachings for a Changing World*, volume 6. Church Publishing, 2017.

De Tocqueville, Alexis. *Democracy in America*. Edited by J. P. Mayer. Translated by George Lawrence. Harper Perennial Modern Classics, 2000.

Drescher, Elizabeth. *Choosing Our Religion: The Spiritual Lives of America's Nones*. Oxford University Press, 2016.

Durkheim, Emile. *The Elementary Forms of Religious Life*. Translated by Joseph W. Swain. Dover Publications, 1912.

Ellwood, Robert. *The Fifties Spiritual Marketplace: American Religion in a Decade of Conflict*. Rutgers University Press, 1997.

Fairless, Caroline. *Children at Worship: Congregations in Bloom.* Church Publishing, 2000.

Finke, Roger, and Rodney Stark. *The Churching of America, 1776–2005: Winners and Losers in Our Religious Economy.* Rutgers University Press, 2005.

Frazer, Gregg. *The Religious Beliefs of America's Founders: Reason, Revelation, and Revolution.* University Press of Kansas, 2012.

Hardegree, Lindsey. "Spirituality in Secular Spaces: Constructing a Practical Missional Ecclesiology." DMin. diss. Candler School of Theology, Spring 2024.

Howland, Grete. *How to Leave Church.* Apocryphile Press, 2024.

Katz, Roberta, et al. *Gen Z, Explained: The Art of Living in a Digital Age.* The University of Chicago Press, 2021.

Main, Darren. *Yoga and the Path of the Urban Mystic.* CreateSpace Publishing Platform, 2002.

McCammon, Sarah. *The Exvangelicals: Loving, Living, and Leaving the Evangelical Church.* St. Martin's Press, 2024.

Mercadante, Linda. *Belief without Borders: Inside the Minds of the Spiritual but not Religious.* Oxford University Press, 2014.

Moynagh, Michael. *Church for Every Context.* SCM Press, 2012.

Odell, Jenny. *How to Do Nothing: Resisting the Attention Economy.* Melville House, 2019.

Putnam, Robert. *Bowling Alone: Revised and Updated: The Collapse and Revival of American Community.* Simon & Schuster, 2001.

Roberts, Elizabeth, and Elias Amidon, eds. *Earth Prayers: 365 Prayers, Poems, and Invocations from Around the World.* HarperOne, 1991.

Roof, Wade Clark, and William McKinney. *American Mainline Religion: Its Changing Shape and Future.* Rutgers University Press, 1987.

Smith, Christian. *Why Religion Went Obsolete: The Demise of Traditional Faith in America.* Oxford University Press, 2025.

Spellers, Stephanie. *The Church Cracked Open: Disruption, Decline, and New Hope for Beloved Community.* Church Publishing, 2021.

Spellers, Stephanie. *Radical Welcome: Embracing God, The Other and the Spirit of Transformation—15th Anniversary Edition.* Morehouse Publishing, 2021.

Springtide Research Institute. *The State of Religion & Young People: Exploring the Sacred,* Springtide, 2023.

Tan, Tay Keong. "Silence, Sacrifice and Shoo-Fly Pies: An Inquiry into the Social Capital and Organizational Strategies of the Amish Community in Lancaster County, Pennsylvania." PhD diss., Harvard University, 1998.

Taylor, Charles. *A Secular Age*. Belknap Press, 2007.

ter Kuile, Casper. *The Power of Ritual: Turning Everyday Activities into Soulful Practices*. HarperOne, 2020.

White, James Emery. *Hybrid Church: Rethinking the Church for a Post-Christian Digital Age*. Zondervan, 2023.

White, James Emery. *The Rise of the Nones: Understanding and Reaching the Religiously Unaffiliated*. Baker Books, 2014.

Yoder, Sue Pizor and Co.lab.inc. *Hear Us Out: Six Questions on Belonging and Belief*. Fortress Press, 2023.

Zscheile, Dwight, and Blair Pogue. *Embracing the Mixed Ecology: Inherited and New Forms of Christian Community Flourishing Together*. Seabury Books, 2025.

Articles

Abramovich, Giselle. "Redefining Health Through Vitality: New Insight into Five Years of Loneliness Trends." The Cigna Group Newsroom. October 2023.

Ammerman, Nancy T. "Spiritual But Not Religious? Beyond Binary Choices in the Study of Religion." *Journal for the Scientific Study of Religion* 52, no. 2 (June 2013): 258–78.

Burge, Ryan. "Just How Bad Is Denominational Decline?" *Religion Unplugged*. June 15, 2023.

Burge, Ryan. "Let's Have a Look at Education and Religious Attendance." *Religion Unplugged*. September 15, 2023.

Burge, Ryan. "The Religious Composition of Political Parties Over the Last 50 Years." *Religion Unplugged*, based on analysis of the General Social Survey 1972–2018. November 7, 2023.

Burge, Ryan. "Religion in 2024: The Plateau Is Real." *Graphs About Religion* (Substack). April 7, 2025.

Christian Leader magazine staff. "Learning from the 'Dones' and 'Nones.'" *Christian Leader*. March 1, 2019.

Cox, Daniel A. "Generation Z and the Future of Faith in America." American Survey Center. March 24, 2022.

Cox, Daniel A., Jacqueline Clemence, and Eleanor O'Neil. "The Decline of Religion in American Family Life." American Enterprise Institute. December 11, 2019.

Cox, Daniel A., and Kelsey Eyre Hammond. "Young Women Are Leaving Church in Unprecedented Numbers." American Survey Center Newsletter. April 4, 2024.

Demerath, N. J. "Cultural Victory and Organizational Defeat in the Paradoxical Decline of Liberal Protestantism." *Journal for the Scientific Study of Religion* 34, no. 4 (December 1995): 458–69.

The Episcopal Church. "Analysis of the 2023 Parochial Report Data."

The Episcopal Church and Ipsos Research. "Jesus in America Survey." March 10, 2022.

The Episcopal Church Evangelism Office. "Hospitality 101: Inviting, Greeting & Incorporating." 2020.

Gallup Organization. "How Religious Are Americans?" March 29, 2024.

Gecewicz, Claire. "'New Age' Beliefs Common Among Both Religious and Nonreligious Americans." Pew Research Center. October 1, 2018.

Global Mission Staff of the Evangelical Lutheran Church in America. "The Accompaniment Model of Mission." *Word & World* 25, no. 1 (Spring 2005).

Graham, Ruth. "In a First Among Christians, Young Men Are More Religious Than Young Women." *The New York Times*. September 25, 2024.

Hout, Michael, and Claude Fischer. "Explaining Why More Americans Have No Religious Preference: Political Backlash and Generational Succession, 1987–2012." *Sociological Science* 1 (October 2014).

Koeth, Stephen. "Postwar Building Boom." *Sacred Architecture Journal* 34 (Fall 2018).

Murthy, Vivek. "Our Epidemic of Loneliness and Isolation: The U.S. Surgeon General's Advisory on the Healing Effects of Social Connection and Community." Office of the U.S. Surgeon General, 2023, 4.

Page, Danielle. "What Happens to Your Brain When You Binge-Watch a TV Series." NBC News, November 4, 2017.

Pepinster, Catherine. "'The Quiet Revival': Huge Increase in Young People Attending Church." Religion Media Centre. April 8, 2025.

Pew Research Center. "Party Identification Among Religious Groups and Religiously Unaffiliated Voters," subhead in "Changing Partisan Coalitions in a Politically Divided Nation." April 9, 2024.

Pew Research Center. "Religious 'Nones' in America: Who They Are and What They Believe." January 24, 2024.

Revell, Rebecca. "Why Don't Young Adults Go to Church Anymore?" *Rebecca Said So* (Blogspot). January 24, 2025.

Sharkey, Patrick. "Homebound: The Long-Term Rise in Time Spent at Home Among U.S. Adults." *Sociological Science* 11, no. 4 (January 2024): 553–78.

Smith, Gregory et al. "Decline of Christianity in the U.S. Has Slowed, May Have Leveled Off: Findings from the 2023–24 Religious Landscape Study." Pew Research Center. February 26, 2025.

Taylor, Rose Schrott. "Pedaling to Spiritual Fitness: How Peloton and Boutique Studios Fill the Void of Modern Religion." *The Presbyterian Outlook*. Last updated October 23, 2024.

Thompson, Derek. "The Anti-Social Century." *The Atlantic Monthly*. February 2025.

Thurston, Angie, and Casper ter Kuile. "How We Gather." Sacred Design Lab. April 2015.

Thurston, Angie, and Casper ter Kuile. "Something More." Sacred Design Lab. November 2019.

Tisby, Jemar. "The 'White' in White Christian Nationalism." *Jemar Tisby, PhD* (Substack). February 22, 2024.

Tucker, Carol. "The 1950s—Powerful Years for Religion." *USC Today*. June 16, 1997.